The Book of

Scenes for Aspiring Actors

Mars

 NTC *Publishing Group*
Lincolnwood, Illinois

To Joy Jacobs

Cover photo: from a production of *Into the Woods,* by Stephen Sondheim and James Lapine, courtesy of the Old Globe Theatre, San Diego, California.

Acknowledgements for interior photos and dramatic selections are listed on page 201, which represents a continuation of the copyright page.

Contents

Introduction

The Book of Scenes for Aspiring Actors was written to acquaint young people with a diversity of scenes, which they can use for a variety of purposes. The first purpose of these scenes is to acquaint them with the language and thought of many different writers throughout history, thus providing a springboard for the study of the periods, the playwrights, and the drama. Second, the scenes can be used as practice for those interested in learning and developing skills in acting and/or directing. They can help in developing character and learning about movement, voice, and placement. Third, because nearly all the scenes involve characters between the ages of twelve and twenty-one, students will have a chance to play roles close to their own ages, which may have more relevance for them than would scenes with older or younger characters.

The scenes range in length from approximately two minutes to ten or twelve minutes. If they so wish, students can start with shorter scenes requiring less time for memorization, and gradually work up to the longer scenes which can be useful for final acting or directing projects. Actors may want to start with two person-scenes and then move on to scenes with multiple characters.

In the introduction to each scene is listed the characters' ages, along with other specific information that can help in preparing the scenes.

It is suggested that students choose different partners for the scenes. That way they will have the experience of acting and reacting with a variety of other performers, each of whom will approach a role a little differently. This type of experience will be valuable to aspiring actors who go on to educational, community, or professional theatre, where actors are used to working with a wide range of people and different approaches to acting.

If the scenes are used by student directors, they should cast their plays differently each time for the same reason—the need to become used to working with a variety of people in a variety of situations.

It is recommended that students perform dramatic scenes from all the historical periods and become acquainted with how they differ in style and presentation. Similarly, students should choose different genres, rather than staying with only the comic or the melodramatic, for instance.

Just as each person approaches a situation or an encounter in life in a different way, so too will students interpret and react individually to each scene in this book. There is no right way of presenting the scenes. There are as many "correct" interpretations as there are performers. There *are* correct rules of presentation, such as projecting the voice so everyone in the classroom or audience can hear. The scenes will provide practice using these rules. But in addition to learning how to act or give a reading, students should receive enjoyment and satisfaction from each scene they choose to present. Theatre, after all, is for enjoyment and entertainment.

Preparing the Scenes

In this book are represented many historical periods and theatrical styles from which you can choose. Since you will be working closely with those scenes you select for interpretation, acting, or directing practice, make certain those dramas are ones you thoroughly enjoy. Of course, your instructor may give you certain requirements, such as choosing a piece from a particular historical period, of a specific length, or with a specific combination of characters, such as two males or two females. Even with limits such as these, you will have several scenes from which to select. To help you, a chart at the end of the book lists each scene, names the characters and their ages, and gives the approximate length of time the scene should take.

Do not select your scene impulsively. If you are selecting the scene for a directing class, take into consideration the actors from whom you will be able to choose and how well you think they can fill the roles.

If you are choosing the scenes for an acting class, get together with the person or persons who will be your partner(s) and spend time together reading through the various possible selections. Try to choose one that you all like. Next, decide who will play each character. You need to give this a lot of thought because not every scene you like will be appropriate for you to play. You may feel uncomfortable with the characters, or you may feel that none of them fits what you want to do or can do. For example, it would be difficult for an eighteen- or twenty-year-old to play the part of Stanley in *A Rosen by Any Other Name* because the character is only twelve years old. It is much easier for a young person to feel comfortable playing an older role, than one that is five or six years younger.

Analyzing the Scene

From the Actor's Viewpoint

Although the following steps in analyzing the piece you've selected are listed in sequence, often you will find that they overlap. For example, it can be difficult to figure out the theme of the scene without knowing the character who is speaking. The steps that follow show the sorts of things you need to consider, but you may want to take them in a different order.

1. Once your selection is final, the next step is to determine why you like the scene. Is it because you identify with the character or because you agree with what he or she is saying? Or maybe you like the humor or the mood. Once you know why you are drawn to the piece, you can try to convey that same feeling to an audience. Of course, you should talk this over with your partner(s) and come to some sort of agreement on how you will present the piece so that your styles of acting are similar. For example, it would not work well if one of you used a broad style of acting—although this might fit such scenes as the one from *The Way of the World*—and the other a more subdued style.

2. What is the mood of the piece? Is it comic or serious? Does it deal with an important subject, and how does the subject affect the mood? This, of course, is tied in with the character's feelings. From what the character is saying, can you figure out how the person feels?

   One you've done this with your own character, get together with your partner(s) and share with each other what you've determined. Be prepared to compromise. Again, this is so the final presentation will be consistent and coherent.

3. Determine the theme of the scene, that is, the central idea or what the writer is saying through the characters. What do you think the playwright most wants to say to an audience? You and your partner(s) need to agree on which character best expresses the playwright's theme and how you can make this clear to your audience.

4. Before getting too far along in the preparation of the scene, you need to analyze your character and to figure out important aspects that will help you portray the person in an effective way. Here are some of the elements you should consider.

   a. Where is the character from? How does this affect his or her feelings, thoughts, and attitudes?

   b. How old is the character? How can you effectively present a person of this age? If the person is younger or older than you, what additional concerns might you have?

   c. What can you tell about the character's environment—geographically, historically, and economically? What is the person's social status? How does all this affect the type of person he or she is?

   d. Similarly, what have been and what are the major influences on the person's life? Sometimes this is easy to determine because the entire scene relates to an issue important to the person. Sometimes, you can only infer specific details about the character.

   e. What are the character's personality traits? How can you tell? How do the traits affect how he or she comes across in the monologue?

   f. What are the character's motives and goals? What does the person hope to accomplish, as far as you can tell by what is said in the scene? Why is he or she reaching for this goal?

   g. Is the person likable? Why or why not? How do you feel about the character? What makes you feel this way?

   h. What sort of relationship does your character have to the others in the scene? How do you know this? Why do you think there is this sort of relationship? How do the characters feel about each other? Why do you think they feel this way?

5. The next step is planning the presentation, and for this you need to take into consideration everything that you have discovered while doing your analysis. First, with your partner(s), figure out what hand and set props (including furniture) you will need, and then decide whether they will be all imaginary, all real, or a mixture. Determine the placement of the furniture. Continue working together in planning the movement and gestures. If you are the type of person who normally uses a lot of gestures and movement

in everyday life, you probably will use more in presenting your scene. But be sure to consider whether your use of gestures matches that of your partner(s). You need to come to agreement on this.

In planning your movement and gestures, you should be guided by several things: (1) the type of person your character is; (2) how you interpret the emotional situation—does it call for more movement, as anger or nervousness might? or less movement, as fright could? and (3) how comfortable you are with gestures.

6. Most likely, you will need to memorize the scene. (In rehearsal, or in reader's theatre, or in some oral interpretation tournament situations, you may be expected to have your script in hand.) Using all the information you have gathered, approach the memorization in whatever way you like. For instance, some actors like to memorize the text before working out movement and gestures; others like to memorize everything at the same time.

Memorizing the scene is an individual process, so what may work well for someone else might not work for you. (1) Make sure you know the meaning of each word and phrase. Although this is important for every type of scene, you may have to research more of the meanings of words and references in historical pieces. (2) Memorize the ideas and the flow of the scene, along with your cues, so that you have the outline or the ideas firmly in mind before you try to memorize exact words. (3) Often it is better to memorize first one sentence, and then a second, which you add to the first, and then a third, and so on, repeating all of your speeches as you add each new sentence. (4) Work on memorizing the scene as the last thing before you go to sleep at night; this helps you retain it.

7. You need to rehearse the scene as many times as necessary to feel confident that you and your partner(s) are presenting it as best you can. Part of this is simply going over and over the scene until you are sure you have it fixed firmly in your mind. To evaluate how the scene is coming across, you may want to have someone videotape it. You can view the tape to assess your scene's strengths and weaknesses, and use it to improve your performance.

Often it is better to write things out so you can be sure you have covered everything important. The analysis sheet that follows can help you. But remember that you do not have to do the sheet in any particular order.

It might be a good idea for you to photocopy the blank sheet, or have your teacher photocopy it for you, so you will have one for each scene in which you are involved.

Character Analysis Sheet

Title of the play: _____

Playwright: _____

Why I chose this scene: _____

_____

Theme or what the scene means to me: _____

_____

_____

Overall mood: _____

My character: _____

    Where from: _____

    Age: _____

    Environment (time and location of scene): _____

_____

    Major influences: _____

    Personality traits: _____

    Motives and goals: _____

    Interests:

        A. Jobs: _____

        B. Hobbies: _____

        C. Friends: _____

How I feel about the character: _____

Relationshp with other characters: _____

_____

Brief description of the other characters: _____

_____

The scenes, of course, can be used for both acting and directing situations.

While a director should analyze each character, it is not necessary to do so as thoroughly as each performer does. A lot of the subtleties of interpretation should be left to the actor, like gestures and facial expressions, unless, of course, the actor is having difficulty with these.

Whether the actors are directing their own scenes or there is a different director, several things are important to know besides those on the actor's analysis sheet.

Every scene in a play has to maintain the audience's interest. The director has to determine what features in his or her scene have the potential to accomplish this. It could be the unusual situation or the unique characters. Often a scene is kept going because of the struggle or conflict. The director needs to know which lines are most important for the audience to grasp in order to understand the struggle (these are called *plot lines*), and which characters are most important at any given second. This way when directors *block the scenes* (plan the movement), they can place the actors where they are the most prominent when they have important lines or actions. This helps the audience focus on what is most vital.

For instance, an actor who is upstage, that is, closer to the back wall of the set, is most prominent as you can see from Figure 1. The other actors in the scene have to look toward this person, thus directing the audience's attention to him or her as well.

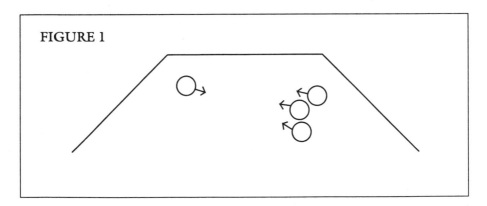

FIGURE 1

A single actor commands more focus than one in a group (see Figure 2).

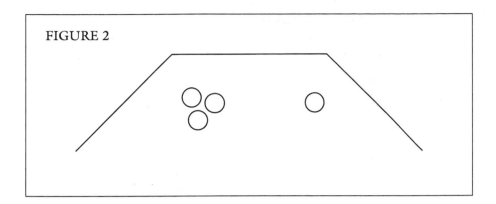

FIGURE 2

In Figure 3, you see how an actor in the center of a line commands attention, particularly if the other actors are looking at him or her.

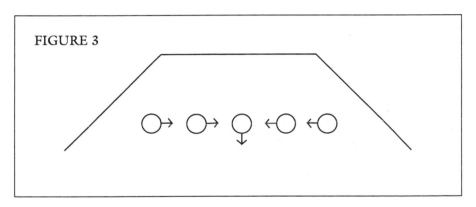

FIGURE 3

Figure 4 shows how an actor who either is standing or is at a higher level on the stage (on a platform, for example) will command more attention than an actor who is seated or who is at a lower level.

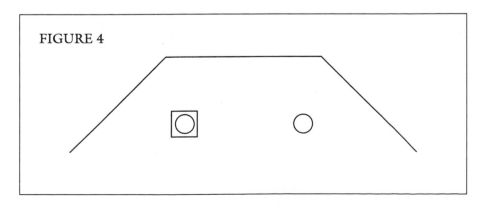

FIGURE 4

It's a good idea for the director to sketch the set as seen from above to be able to keep in mind, when planning the movement, where the furniture or other set props are placed. A sample sketch can be seen in Figure 5.

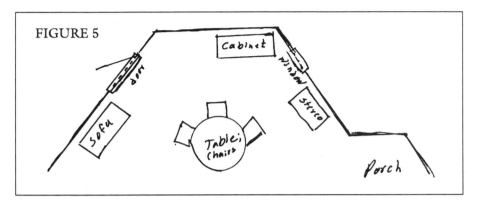

FIGURE 5

As a director, you may choose to fill out an analysis sheet like the one that follows.

You should also prepare a *prompt book,* that is, the script photocopied in the center of an 8½" x 11" sheet of paper, so there is plenty of space in the margins to write anything important having to do with the movement or placement of the actors. This can be done with drawings of the set showing the movement, by written directions, or even with a combination of drawing and writing, as shown in Figure 6.

Often a director will want to go back and change things, so it is better to write in pencil, rather than pen.

Similarly, the director should instruct the actors to carry a pencil so they can record blocking instructions in their texts.

Director's Analysis

Title of the play: _____

Playwright: _____

Theme or central idea: _____

_____

Character's descriptions:

    A. Character 1: _____

    _____

    B. Character 2: _____

    _____

    C. Character 3: _____

    _____

    D. Character 4: _____

    _____

    E. Character 5: _____

    _____

Goals of each character: _____

_____

_____

_____

_____

Why each character is included: _____

_____

_____

_____

_____

Director's Analysis, page 2

How each character advances the scene: _____

_____

_____

_____

_____

The basic struggle or conflict of the scene: _____

_____

_____

_____

_____

The needs of each character: _____

_____

_____

_____

_____

Diagram of the set, showing placement of set pieces, such as furniture, trees, rocks, and so on:

FIGURE 6

(handwritten: desk, B.D., chair, drawer, T B)

(As the lights come up, TIMOTHY is kneeling by one of the two single beds, hands clasped, resting on the mattress. He doesn't glance up as BOB enters, carrying two suitcases.)

TIMOTHY: (Praying) Our Thomas Wolfe, who art in heaven, hallowed be thy name. Thy novels be read; thy writing be loved in the rest of earth as it is in Carolina.

(Astounded, BOB stops for a moment and then crosses to the other bed. He turns, keeping an eye on TIMOTHY.)

TIMOTHY: Give us this day our daily prose, and forgive us our writing blocks as we forgive your critics. *(handwritten: He sits, on the bed.)*

(BOB sets down his suitcases, shaking his head.)

TIMOTHY: (Rising and facing BOB, he grins.) There's no god. No heaven, except what we create in our minds. Thomas Wolfe is my god. (He holds out his hand) I'm Timothy U. Landis. *(handwritten: As T. holds out his hand, Bob rises.)*

BOB: (Taking his hand.) Hi, Bob Thompson.

(handwritten: T. (crosses) to his bed and sits in the center.)

TIMOTHY: Since I arrived first, I took this side of the room, this bed, this half of the dresser. (He points to a large, squat chest of drawers.)

BOB: Fine, I have no preference. *(handwritten: Placing a suitcase on the bed.)*

TIMOTHY: Each one of us has preferences. We simply have to find what they are and not deny them. We have to be true to ourselves. *(handwritten: T. rises), pulls out his desk chair and straddles it, facing Bob.)*

BOB: (Placing ~~the other~~ suitcases atop a student desk by the bed.) Maybe that's why I'm here. To find out my preferences, what I want out of life. (He opens the suitcase and pulls out socks and underwear, shoving them into drawers.) *(handwritten: (Crosses to the dresser.))*

TIMOTHY: Need any help?

BOB: (Surprised.) You can hang these up, if you like. (He hands shirts and jeans to TIMOTHY.)

TIMOTHY: (Taking the clothes to the closet) I'm aware of my preferences. All of them. I know what I want. (He drapes a shirt around a hanger, shaping it just right so there are no wrinkles.) *(handwritten: (He turns to face T.))*

BOB: That's wonderful. But if that's the case, why are you even here?

(handwritten: (Facing Bob) turns and)

TIMOTHY: Scoff, if you want to. (He hangs up the pants.) But I'm going to be a writer. (He sighs deeply.) I may

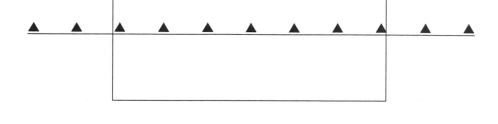

Scenes for One Male and One Female

Whitney: 18 (male)
Carlyle: 18 (female)
Length of scene: Three minues and 30 seconds
to four minutes and 30 seconds

The Stonewater Rapture

Doug Wright/ *U.S.A.*

Doug Wright's first published play, *The Stonewater Rapture*, takes a humorous look at adolescents growing into sexual awareness, the embarrassment this can cause, and the serious problems that can result.

Although the subject is treated lightly, the content is far from humorous. Beyond this point in the play, the audience discovers that both Whitney and Carlyle, in a way, are misfits, who are forced to lie to themselves in order to face up to life.

CARLYLE: Whitney, Ted Pewter was the only other boy who had a chance and he's guilty of the sin of pride. Look at the way he blow dries his hair.

WHITNEY: I don't want to be president.

CARLYLE: How do you think that makes me feel?

Whitney: I'm glad you got secretary. Carlyle, I'm not going to be a preacher.

CARLYLE: Getting president doesn't mean you have to be a preacher.

WHITNEY: You want to see something?

(*Whitney crosses to the desk and pulls out a thin stack of papers. He hands it to Carlyle*)

CARLYLE: You didn't tell me you were applying to seminary school! Whitney, I think that's wonderful. Look. You typed all the answers.

WHITNEY: My Dad filled it out for me. He wrote all the essays to make sure I wouldn't tell them I was Hindu or something. Now all it needs is my signature, then it goes in the mail, and WHAM! I'm behind a pulpit.

CARLYLE: They might not accept you.

WHITNEY: I was just voted president of the Youth Ministry. It's the kiss of death.

CARLYLE: It doesn't mean you'll get in. It takes a lot more to be a good preacher. You have to be blessed with strength and faith and love for your fellow man . . .

WHITNEY: There's something more.

CARLYLE: What?

WHITNEY: You have to be a good public speaker. I suck.

CARLYLE: You're not so awful.

WHITNEY: You saw me this afternoon.

CARLYLE: You knew if you won, you'd have to make a speech. You should've had one ready.

WHITNEY: I did. My father gave me this whole five-page speech on the positive power of prayer in adolescence. It was right in my back pocket. But you saw. I practically fainted, all because of the word "puberty." I couldn't stand up there and say "puberty" in front of all those ladies. They would've choked on their egg salad. I suck.

CARLYLE: Then they probably won't take you.

WHITNEY: They'll take me. I make all *A's* and my uncle is on the board.

CARLYLE: Mama says you have the calling.

WHITNEY: Dad says there are only two honorable professions in the world: carpentry and preaching. I made him a tie rack for his birthday and the wood split. That's my calling.

CARLYLE: Where are your folks?

WHITNEY: Cleaning up after the picnic. Then they're teaching that singles seminar on "Finding a Mate Through God." Dad says a lot of nice bachelors show up. He thinks your mom should give it a try.

CARLYLE: Can we go out on the porch?

WHITNEY: It's hotter than hell and there are mosquitoes.

CARLYLE: You shouldn't have me over if your parents aren't here.

(*She leads him out onto the porch*)

WHITNEY: We've been seeing each other for two months now and I'm still afraid I'll get a face full of tear gas if I brush up against your knee.

CARLYLE: Whitney, I've made a list of the things we should start doing. (*Whitney groans*) First, we're going to start making those Wednesday night sing-a-longs at the nursing home mandatory attendance for the whole group. I feel stupid singing all by myself. It keeps the old people from joining in. They think it's a solo. Miss Willoughby, she tries to help out, but whenever she sings it's always the wrong song. I could be singing the Doxology, and she still thinks it's "Indian Love Call." It embarrasses everybody, but she refuses to wear her hearing aid. Second, I'm sick and tired of the way some people come to the Fellowship parties for the food and not the faith. It makes us look bad. Part of that is your responsibility. If you'd try harder to attract people at school . . .

WHITNEY: I was going to go out for the football team, but that's shot to hell now. I can't be at practice and Bible Study at the same time.

CARLYLE: Your legs are too skinny. You'd get bulldozed.

WHITNEY: They are not.

CARLYLE: You could soak your feet in a Coke bottle.

WHITNEY: Cut it out. I've been eating more.

CARLYLE: Let me see.

WHITNEY: No.

CARLYLE: Come on. Please.

WHITNEY: Uh-uh.

CARLYLE: You told me you hated football. I don't know why you want to play now.

WHITNEY: Everybody plays..

CARLYLE: Who?

WHITNEY: Arthur Horrishill and Michael MaCaffey.

CARLYLE: But they're mean to you.

WHITNEY: No, they're not.

CARLYLE: Yesterday they put Vaseline all over your steering wheel.

WHITNEY: It was a joke.

CARLYLE: You zig-zagged all the way home.

WHITNEY: It was funny. Anyway, if I was on the team, do you think they'd do that?

CARLYLE: But you're better than they are. Mama says you're the only decent boy for miles. She'd rather talk to you than most people her own age. She says boys like Arthur and Michael have one-track minds that lead straight to hell, and knives where their flesh should be, but not you.

Questions for Discussion

1. How would you describe the type of person Carlyle is? Whitney? Point to lines in the script that back up what you say.

2. What sorts of problems can you see that Whitney has? Why does he want to play football? Why does he say that the Vaseline was put on his steering wheel as a joke?

3. This scene is more revealing of Whitney's problems than Carlyle's. Yet the author hints at her problems as well. Can you see what they might be?

4. Do you sympathize with Whitney? With Carlyle? Why? Can you identify with their problems and feelings? In what way?

5. Can you see any ways in which Carlyle is trying to help Whitney in this scene? Explain.

Wilfred: 16
Caroline: "Very young," which probably means 15 or 16
Length of scene: Four minutes and 30 seconds to five minutes and 30 seconds

Secret Service

William Gillette / *U.S.A.*

The Union Army is threatening Richmond. Two brothers, members of the secret service, are to seize control of the telegraph office and send false orders to the commander of the Confederate Army, thus allowing Union forces to capture Richmond.

This scene occurs in the first act, after Wilfred already has decided he is going to go fight for the Confederate Army. He hopes to join his father, a division commander.

Here, of course, it seems that one big reason he wants to fight is to gain Caroline's attention, if not her love.

The play, a melodrama, was first performed in 1895 in Philadelphia, with William Gillette (the author) playing the leading role.

WILFRED: (*Coldly*) Good evening, Miss Mitford! (*Emphasize "Miss Mitford"*) (*Both now start rapidly toward door up* L. C., *but as it brings them toward each other, they stop simultaneously up* L. *in order to avoid meeting in the doorway*)

CAROLINE: Excuse me—I'm in a *great* hurry!

WILFRED: That's plain enough! (*Looks at her*) Another party I reckon! (*"Party" with contemptuous emphasis*)

CAROLINE: You reckon perfectly correct—it *is* another party! (*Turns and moves slowly down toward* C.)

WILFRED: Dancing! (*Moves down* L. C.)

CAROLINE: Well—what of it! What's the matter with dancing I'd like to know!

WILFRED: (L. C.) Nothing's the matter with it—if you want to *do* it! (*Stands looking away to down* L.)

CAROLINE: Well I want to *do* it fast enough if that's all you mean! (*Turns away a little toward* R.)

WILFRED: (*An emphatic turn toward her*) But I must say it's a pretty way to carry on—with the sound of the cannon not six miles away!

(WILFRED *is dead in earnest not only in this scene but throughout the entire performance. To give the faintest idea that he thinks there is anything humorous about his lines or behavior would be inexcusable*)

CAROLINE: (*Turning back to him*) Well what do you want us to do—sit down and cry about it?—A heap o' good *that* would do now wouldn't it?

WILFRED: Oh—I haven't time to talk about it! (*Turns up as if to go*)

CAROLINE: Well it was you who started *out* to talk about it—I'm right sure *I* didn't!

(WILFRED *stops dead on* CAROLINE'S *speech , and after a quick glance to see that no one is near, goes down to her*)

WILFRED: You needn't try to fool me! I know well enough how you've been carrying on since our engagement was broken off! Half a dozen officers proposing to you—a dozen for all I know!

CAROLINE: What difference does it make! I haven't got to *marry* 'em have I?

WILFRED: (L.C.) Well—(*Twist of head*) it isn't very nice to go on like that I must say—proposals by the wholesale! (*Turning away*)

CAROLINE: (c.) Goodness gracious—what's the use of talking to me about it? *They're* the ones that propose—*I* don't!

WILFRED: (*Turning on her* L.C.) Well what do you let 'em *do* it for?

CAROLINE: (C.) How can I help it?

WILFRED: Ho! (*Sneer*) Any girl can help it!—You helped it with *me* all right!

CAROLINE: Well—(*An odd little glance to floor in front*) that was different!

WILFRED: And ever since you threw me ovah—

CAROLINE: (*Looking up at him indignantly*) Oh!—I *didn't* throw you ovah—you just *went* ovah! (*Turns away to* R. *a little*)

WILFRED: Well I went over because you walked off alone with Major Sillsby that night we were at Drury's Bluff an' encouraged him to propose—(CAROLINE *looks round in wrath*) Yes—(*Advancing to* C.) *encouraged* him!

CAROLINE: (R. C.) Of *co'se* I did! I didn't want 'im hangin' round forever did I? That's the on'y way to finish 'em off!

WILFRED: (C.) You want to finish too many of 'em off! Nearly every officer in the 17th Virginyah, I'll be sworn!

CAROLINE: Well what do you want me to do—string a placard round my neck saying "No proposals received here—apply at the office!" Would that make you feel any better?

WILFRED: (*Throwing it off with pretended carelessness*) Oh—it doesn't make any difference to me what you do! (*Turns away*)

CAROLINE: Well if it doesn't make any difference to you, it doesn't make as much as that to me! (*Turns and goes to couch at* R. C. *and sits on left end of it*)

WILFRED: (*Turning on her again*) Oh—it doesn't! I think it *does* though!—You looked as if you enjoyed it pretty well while the 3rd Virginyah was in the city!

CAROLINE: (*Jumping to her feet*) Enjoyed it! I should think I did! I just love every one of 'em! They're on their way to the front! They're going to fight for us—an'—an' die for us—an' I *love* 'em! (*Turns front*)

WILFRED: Well why don't you accept one of 'em an' done with it!

CAROLINE: How do you know but what I'm going to?

WILFRED: (*Goes toward her a little*) I suppose it'll be one of those *smart* young fellows with a cavalry uniform!

CAROLINE: It'll be *some* kind of a uniform—I can tell you that! It won't be anybody that stays here in Richmond—

WILFRED: (*Unable for a few seconds to say anything. Looks about room helplessly. Then speaks in low voice*) Now I see what it was! I had to stay in Richmond—an' so you—an' so—

CAROLINE: (*In front of couch* R. C.) Well—(*Looking down—playing with something with her foot*) that made a heap o' difference! (*Looks up.—Different tone*) Why I was the on'y girl on Franklin Street that didn't have a—a—(*Hesitates*)—someone she was engaged to at the front! The on'y one! Just *think* what it was to be out of it like that! (WILFRED *simply looks at her*) Why you've no idea what I suffered! Besides, it's our—it's our *duty* to help all we can!

WILFRED: (*Looking up toward front*) Help! (*Thinking of the trousers under his coat*)

CAROLINE: Yes—help! There aren't many things we girls can do—I know that well enough! But Colonel Woodbridge—he's one o' Morgan's men you know—well he told Mollie Pickens that the boys fight *twice* as well when they have a—a sweetheart at home! (WILFRED *glances quickly about as he thinks*)

WILFRED: He said *that* did he!

CAROLINE: Yes—an' if we can make 'em fight twice as well why we just ought to do it—that's all! We girls can't do much but we can do *something!*

WILFRED: (*Short pause.—He makes an absent-minded motion of feeling of the package under his arm*) You're in earnest, are you?

CAROLINE: Earnest!

WILFRED: You really want to help—all you can!

CAROLINE: Well I should think I *did!*

WILFRED: Yes—but do you *now?*

CAROLINE: Of co'se—that's what I say!

WILFRED: An' if I was—(*Glances around cautiously*)—if I was going to join the army—would you help *me?*

CAROLINE: (*Looking front and down.—Slight embarrassment*) Why of co'se I would—if it was anything I could do! (*Emphasize "do" slightly*)

WILFRED: (*Earnestly—quite near her*) Oh it's something you can *do* all right!

CAROLINE: (R. C.—*Hardly daring to look up*) What is it?

WILFRED: (*Unrolling a pair of old gray army trousers, taking them from under his coat so that they unfurl before her on cue*) Cut these off! (*Short pause—*CAROLINE *looking at trousers—*WILFRED *looking at her.* WILFRED *soon goes on very earnestly, holding trousers before his own legs to measure*) They're about twice too long! All you got to do is to cut 'em off about there, an' sew up the ends so they won't ravel out!

CAROLINE: (R. C.—*The idea beginning to dawn on her*) Why they're for the Army! (*Taking trousers and hugging them to her—legs hanging down*)

WILFRED: (C.) Sh!—Don't speak so loud for heaven's sake! (*A glance back as if afraid of being overheard*) I've got a jacket here too! (*Shows her a small army coat*) Nearly a fit—came from the hospital—Johnny Seldon wore it—he won't want it any more you know—an' he was just about my size!

CAROLINE: (R. C.—*Low voice*) No—he won't want it any more. (*Stands thinking*)

WILFRED: (C.—*After a slight pause*) Well!—What is it!—I thought you said you wanted to help!

CAROLINE: (*Quickly*) I do! I do!

Questions for Discussion

1. Point out and explain the humorous aspects of this scene.

2. Why is Wilfred so upset with Caroline? Does he have a right to be? Why?

3. Is Wilfred a typical teenager? What makes you think so? Why do you think he wants so much to join the Confederate Army?

4. Why do you suppose Caroline has become engaged to so many people? Is this logical?

5. If you met Caroline and Wilfred in real life, would you like them? Why?

Millamant: Probably about 18 (female)
Mirabell: Probably 20 to 22 (male)
Length of scene: Five minutes and 15 seconds
to six minutes and 15 seconds

The Way of the World

William Congreve/*England*

Written in 1700, this play is about the wooing of Millamant by Mirabell. This scene, in which the two set forth the conditions that will make their marriage acceptable and tolerable, is the highpoint of the play. Restoration comedy, such as this, is called comedy of manners because it deals with the upper class's concerns with the latest in fashion, arranged marriage, witty repartee, and a preoccupation with seduction. This sort of play requires a polished and graceful style of acting.

Congreve is usually considered one of the best at writing Restoration comedy, and *The Way of the World* is most often considered the best play of its type.

MIRABELL: Do you lock yourself up from me, to make my search more curious? Or is this pretty artifice contrived to signify that here the chase must end, and my pursuit be crowned, for you can fly no further?

MILLAMANT: Vanity! No—I'll fly and be followed to the last moment. Though I am upon the very verge of matrimony, I expect you should solicit me as much as if I were wavering at the gate of a monastery, with one foot over the threshold. I'll be solicited to the very last, nay, and afterwards.

MIRABELL: What, after the last?

MILLAMANT: Oh, I should think I was poor and had nothing to bestow, if I were reduced to an inglorious ease, and freed from the agreeable fatigues of solicitation.

MIRABELL: But do not you know, that when favors are conferred upon instant and tedious solicitation, that they diminish in their value, and that both the giver loses the grace, and the receiver lessens his pleasure?

MILLAMANT: It may be in things of common application, but never sure in love. Oh, I hate a lover that can dare to think he draws a moment's air independent on the bounty of his mistress. There is not so impudent a thing in nature as the saucy look of an assured man, confident of success. The pedantic arrogance of a very husband has not so pragmatical an air. Ah! I will never marry, unless I am first made sure of my will and pleasure.

MIRABELL: Would you have 'em both before marriage? Or will you be contented with the first now, and stay for the other till after grace?

MILLAMANT: Ah, don't be impertinent.—My dear liberty, shall I leave thee? My faithful solitude, my darling contemplation, must I bid you then adieu? Ay-h, adieu—my morning thoughts, agreeable wakings, indolent slumbers, all ye *douceurs,* ye *sommeils du matin,*[1] adieu?—I can't do't, 'tis more than impossible. Positively, Mirabell, I'll lie abed in a morning as long as I please.

MIRABELL: Then I'll get up in a morning as early as I please.

MILLAMANT: Ah! Idle creature, get up when you will. —And d'ee hear, I

---

[1] all ye sweetness, ye slumbers of the morning.

won't be called names after I'm married; positively I won't be called names.

MIRABELL: Names?

MILLAMANT: Ay, as wife, spouse, my dear, joy, jewel, love, sweetheart, and the rest of the nauseous cant, in which men and their wives are so fulsomely familiar—I shall never bear that.—Good Mirabell, don't let us be familiar or fond, nor kiss before folks, like my Lady Fadler and Sir Francis; nor go to Hyde Park together the first Sunday in a new chariot, to provoke eyes and whispers, and then never to be seen together again, as if we were proud of one another the first week, and ashamed of one another for ever after. Let us never visit together, nor go to a play together, but let us be very strange and well bred. Let us be as strange as if we had been married a great while, and as well bred as if we were not married at all.

MIRABELL: Have you any more conditions to offer? Hitherto your demands are pretty reasonable.

MILLAMANT: Trifles,—as liberty to pay and receive visits to and from whom I please; to write and receive letters, without interrogatories or wry faces on your part. To wear what I please, and choose conversation with regard only to my own taste; to have no obligation upon me to converse with wits that I don't like, because they are your acquaintance; or to be intimate with fools, because they may be your relations. Come to dinner when I please, dine in my dressing-room when I'm out of humor, without giving a reason. To have my closet inviolate; to be sole empress of my tea-table, which you must never presume to approach without first asking leave. And lastly, wherever I am, you shall always knock at the door before you come in. These articles subscribed, if I continue to endure you a little longer, I may by degrees dwindle into a wife.

MIRABELL: You bill of fare is something advanced in this latter account. Well, have I liberty to offer conditions—that when you are dwindled into a wife I may not be beyond measure enlarged into a husband?

MILLAMANT: You have free leave; propose your utmost; speak and spare not.

MIRABELL: I thank you. *Imprimis*[2] then, I convenant that your acquain-

---

[2] in the first place.

tance be general; that you admit no sworn confidant or intimate of your own sex; no she-friend to screen her affairs under your countenance and tempt you to make trial of a mutual secrecy. No decoy-duck to wheedle you a fop-scrambling to the play in a mask[3]—then bring you home in a pretended fright, when you think you shall be found out—and rail at me for missing the play and disappointing the frolic which you had, to pick me up and prove my constancy.

MILLAMANT: Detestable *imprimis!* I go to the play in a mask!

MIRABELL: *Item,* I article, that you continue to like your own face as long as I shall; and while it passes current with me, that you endeavor not to new-coin it. To which end, together with all vizards for the day, I prohibit all masks for the night, made of oiled-skins and I know not what—hog's bones, hare's gall, pig-water, and the marrow of a roasted cat. In short, I forbid all commerce with the gentlewoman in What-d'ye-call-it Court. *Item,* I shut my doors against all bawds with baskets, and pennyworths of muslin, china, fans, atlases, etc.—*Item,* when you shall be breeding—

MILLAMANT: Ah! name it not.

MIRABELL: Which may be presumed, with a blessing on our endeavors—

MILLAMANT: Odious endeavors!

MIRABELL: I denounce against all strait lacing, squeezing for a shape, till you mold my boy's head like a sugar-loaf, and instead of a man-child, make me the father of a crooked billet.[4] Lastly, to the dominion of the tea-table I submit,—but with proviso, that you exceed not in your province; but restrain yourself to native and simple tea-table drinks, as tea, chocolate, and coffee, as likewise to genuine and authorized tea-table talk—such as mending of fashions, spoiling reputations, railing at absent friends, and so forth—but that on no account you encroach upon the men's prerogative, and presume to drink healths, or toast fellows; for prevention of which I banish all foreign forces, all auxiliaries to the tea-table, as orange-brandy, all aniseed, cinnamon, citron, and Barbadoes waters, together with ratafia and the most noble spirit, clary,—but for cowslip wine, poppy

---

[3] no sneaking off to the opera, disguised, with "flashy men."
[4] warped block of wood.

water, and all dormitives, those I allow. These provisos admitted, in other things I may prove a tractable and complying husband.

MILLAMANT: Oh, horrid provisos! Filthy strong waters! I toast fellows, other men! I hate your odious provisos.

MIRABELL: Then we're agreed. Shall I kiss your hand upon the contract?

Questions for Discussion

1. How would you feel if you were asked to enter into a premarital agreement such as this?

2. This scene is considered among the best examples of Restoration comedy. Why do you think that is true? Do you like it? Why?

3. What is your opinion of Mirabell? Of Millamant? Explain.

4. Which of the demands made by Mirabell or Millamant do you consider the most outrageous? Why?

5. Why do you suppose this type of drama was so popular during the Restoration? (You may need to research the political and social climate of England during the 1600s and 1700s.)

Nadia: Age unspecified
John: Age unspecified
Length of scene: Three minutes to three
minutes and 30 seconds

The Wrong Man

Laura Harrington/*U.S.A.*

This play is complete in itself and was presented for the first
time as part of an evening of five-minute plays at New
Dramatists, a service organization for playwrights that has
the aim of encouraging and developing playwriting in America.
This piece and others from New Dramatists were published
by Broadway Play Publishing in *Short Pieces from the New
Dramatists*.

The acting should be light, giving it almost a feeling of
fantasy, with a bare touch of the serious every now and then.

(*A party,* NADIA *is alone on the balcony, dancing.* JOHN *enters, watches* NADIA *and begins dancing with her. She dances with him for a beat or two, then turns her back on him.*)

JOHN: Excuse me—

NADIA: (*Turning to face him.*) No . . . We're not going to do that.

JOHN: I just wanted to know—

NADIA: —My name.

JOHN: Right.

NADIA: I've done that before. You've done that before. Tonight we're going to do something new . . . Instead of the usual banalities we're going to lie to each other.

JOHN: Oh, sure.

NADIA: About the last time we met—

JOHN: What are you talking about?

NADIA: The last time we met. Which was the first time. That's where we start.

JOHN: The first time . . . ?

NADIA: Before anything happened.

JOHN: (*Sarcastic*) Right. Before anything happened.

NADIA: You've got it now.

JOHN: You're serious about this.

NADIA: Very.

(*A beat*)

JOHN: I'm not sure I know how to do this.

NADIA: It's easy. Believe me.

(*Pause*)

JOHN: Okay . . . Okay . . . It was a party . . .

NADIA: A dance.

JOHN: A party, a dance . . . You were dancing.

NADIA: I could feel you watching me.

JOHN: I had been watching you for a very long time.

NADIA: I was careful near you . . .

JOHN: A summer night.

NADIA: Late summer.

JOHN: You sat next to another girl who turned to you and said: "You're very beautiful" . . . and you laughed.

NADIA: I'd been drinking . . . it was a party . . .

JOHN: A dance.

NADIA: And I'd been dancing . . .

JOHN: You sat next to me. Very close. Your thigh lay pressed against mine . . . I felt that I could almost, not quite, touch your breast . . .

NADIA: I was heady with liquor, with the night, with the surprise of your heat, with this girl telling me I was beautiful . . . I looked up, you were reaching your arms out to pull me to my feet, and I thought . . . "He is going to pick me right up out of my skin."

JOHN: I'd never touched you.

NADIA: I'd never touched you and I thought that you would pull me straight out of my skin.

JOHN: Your dress was a fine fabric, almost as fine as your skin . . . your shoulders—I ran my hands across your shoulders. I lifted your hair and put my hand to the nape of your neck.

NADIA: This was the first time . . .

JOHN: Yes.

NADIA: I was facing you. I was cold. We were children.

JOHN: No. A hot summer night. By the ocean.

NADIA: Near enough to smell the sea.

JOHN: We were no longer children.

NADIA: We came inside to dance.

JOHN: We weren't touching. Just dancing close. You were laughing . . . I watched the pulse at the base of your throat . . .

NADIA: I wondered what you would do, how you would do it . . . whether you would promise me things.

JOHN: I talked to you. I was so terrified that I couldn't stop talking . . . all of the things that I told you about . . . from the first time I'd seen you and been afraid to speak.

NADIA: No. You didn't say a word. We were walking, along the beach, not saying anything. And you kissed me. Startled me.

JOHN: I told you I would love you always.

NADIA: We lay down. You put your head on my breast. I pushed you away. Not like that. Not like a child coming to his mother.

JOHN: No. I talked until I had no breath left. I promised you everything I could think of. We were by the road, walking in the roadside. I couldn't stop talking until you kissed me . . . You pushed me by a fence. You put your hands inside my shirt . . . I was afraid to touch you.

NADIA: It was a beach

JOHN: Another man, another time.

NADIA: No. (*She moves toward him*) You pulled me out of my skin. When I stood up I was a new person.

JOHN: (*Backing off*) But I've never touched you.

NADIA: And I don't know your name.

(*A beat*)

JOHN: Right.

(*A beat*)

NADIA: It's just as well.

JOHN: Yes. Just as well.

(JOHN *exits*)

Questions for Discussion

1. Why do you suppose Nadia wants to have a "pretend" conversation rather than a real one?

2. From what Nadia says here, can you tell anything about the type of person she is? Explain. Do the same for John's character.

3. Why do you suppose Nadia turns her back on John after dancing with him for only a short time? What are his feelings at that point? Explain.

4. Do you think things like this ever happen in real life? Why?

5. Why do you suppose Nadia and John agree on some things about the time they supposedly met and disagree on others?

Paula: A "lovely, young girl," probably about 20

Will: A "serious boy," probably also 20 or 21

Length of scene: Four minutes and 30 seconds to five minutes and 30 seconds.

End of Summer

S. N. Behrman / U.S.A.

Although Behrman came from a middle-class family, his plays typically deal with the upper class. A number of them, such as *End of Summer,* deal with a conflict of ideas and political beliefs, reflecting the tensions of the Depression era through World War II.

Overall, the play, which premiered in 1936, has little in the way of action, but it has excellent and well-differentiated characters. Paula is a daughter of wealthy parents; Will is a radical from a lower social scale. This scene shows that Paula and Will have a close relationship, even though Will doubts that Paula believes in social reform as strongly as he does.

PAULA: What a conquest you've made of Granny! Way and ahead of all my beaus!

WILL: That undistinguished mob! Who couldn't?

PAULA: As long as you admit there is a mob . . .

WILL: Why wouldn't there be? Everybody loves you for your money!

PAULA (*confidently*): I know it! And of all the fortune-hunters I've had dangling after me you're easily the most . . .

WILL: Blatant!

PAULA: That's it! Blatant! Like my new slacks?

WILL: Love 'em.

PAULA: Love me?

WILL: Loathe you.

PAULA: Good! Kiss? (*They kiss quickly*)

WILL: Funny thing about your grandmother . . .

PAULA: Now I won't have you criticizing Granny . . .

WILL: I'm crazy about her. You feel she's been through everything and that she understands everything. Not this though. Not the essential difference between her times and ours.

PAULA: Oh dear! Is it the end of the world then?

WILL: The end of this world.

PAULA(*goes to window seat right, with sigh*): Such a pretty world. (*She points through windows at the garden and sea beyond*) Look at it! Too bad it has to go! Meantime before it quite dissolves let's go for a swim. (*She starts for door*)

WILL (*abstracted*): All right . . . (*Following her to window seat*)

PAULA (*she turns back*): What's on your mind?

WILL: Wanted to speak to you about something . . .

PAULA: What?

WILL (*embarrassed slightly*): Er—your mother . . .

PAULA: What's Mother gone and done now? Out with it. Or is it you? My boyfriends are always in love with Mother. I've had to contend with that all my life. So if it's that you needn't even mention it . . . come on.

WILL: No but really, Paula . . .

PAULA: Well then, out with it! What is it!

WILL: This. (*He gives her note*) Found it on my breakfast tray this morning in a sealed envelope marked "Confidential."

PAULA (*reading note aloud, rather bewildered*): "To give my little girl a good time with, Leonie Frothingham."

WILL: And this! (*He hands her check.* PAULA *takes it and looks at it.*)

PAULA: A hundred dollars. Does Mother think her little girl can have a good time with *that*? She doesn't know her little girl!

WILL: But what'll I do with it? How'll I get it back to her?

PAULA: Over my dead body you'll get it back to her! You'll spend it on Mother's little girl. Now come on swimming!

WILL: Does your mother put one of these on every breakfast tray?

PAULA: Argue it out with her.

WILL: I can't. It would seem ungracious. You must give it back to her for me.

PAULA: Catch me! Don't take it too seriously. She slips all the kids something every once in a while. She knows my friends are all stony. You overestimate the importance of money, Will—it's a convenience, that's all. You've got a complex on it.

WILL: I have! I've got to have. It's all right to be dainty about money when you've lots of it as you have . . .

PAULA: Rotten with it is the expression, I believe . . .

WILL: I repudiate that expression. It is genteel and moralistic. You can't be rotten with money—you can only be *alive* with it.

PAULA: You and the rest of our crowd make me feel it's bad taste to be rich. But what can I do? I didn't ask for it!

WILL: I know. But look here . . . I've got a brother out of college two years who's worked six weeks in that time and is broke and here I am in an atmosphere with hundred-dollar bills floating around!

PAULA (*with check*): Send him that!

WILL: Misapplication of funds!

PAULA (*warmly*): Mother would be only too . . .

WILL: I know she would—but that isn't the point . . . You know, Paula—

PAULA: What?

WILL: Sometimes I think if we weren't in love with each other we
should be irreconcilable enemies—

PAULA: Nothing but sex, eh?

WILL: That's all.

PAULA: In that case—(*They kiss*)

WILL: That's forgiving. But seriously, Paula—

PAULA: Seriously what?

WILL: I can't help feeling I'm here on false pretenses. What am I doing
with a millionaire family—with you? If your mother knew what I
think, and what I've let you in for in college—she wouldn't touch
me with a ten-foot pole. And you too—I'm troubled about the
superficiality of your new opinions. Isn't your radicalism—acquired
coloring?

PAULA: I hope not. But—so is all education.

WILL: I know but—!

PAULA: What are you bleating about? Didn't I join you on that expedi-
tion to Kentucky to be treated by that sovereign state as an offensive
foreigner? My back aches yet when I remember that terrible bus ride.
Didn't I get my name in the papers picketing? Didn't I give up my
holiday to go with you to the Chicago Peace Congress? Didn't I?

WILL (*doubtfully*): Yes, you did.

PAULA: But you're not convinced. Will darling, don't you realize that
since knowing you and your friends, since I've, as you say, acquired
your point of view about things, my life has had an excitement and a
sense of reality it's never had before. I've simply come alive—that's
all! Before then I was bored—terribly bored without knowing why. I
wanted something more—fundamental—without knowing what.
You've made me see. I'm terribly grateful to you, Will darling. I
always shall be.

WILL: You are a dear, Paula, and I adore you—but—

PAULA: Still unconvinced?

WILL: This money of yours. What'll it do to us?

PAULA: I'll turn it over to you. Then you can give me an allowance—
and save your pride.

WILL: I warn you, Paula—

PAULA: What?

WILL: If you turn it over to me, I'll use it in every way I can to make it impossible for anyone to have so much again.

PAULA: That's all right with me, Will.

WILL: Sometimes you make me feel I'm taking candy from babies.

PAULA: The candy is no good for the baby, anyway. Besides, let's cross that bridge when we come to it.

Questions for Discussion

1. Why do you suppose Paula is at least halfheartedly embracing the same causes as Will?

2. Do you think their relationship has a chance to continue? Why?

3. What do you think are Paula's real views about having money? Will's?

4. In this play Will is a guest at Paula's home. Do you think it likely that an upper-class family would invite a radical as a houseguest? Why?

5. Why do you think Will has such strong views about social reform?

Annie: a young woman
Tommy: Annie's friend
Length of scene: Five minutes and 30 seconds
to six minutes and 30 seconds

My Friend Never Said Goodbye

Robert Mauro/ *U.S.A.*

This following scene is from a two-character play about the aftermath of a friend's suicide. The characters are Annie and Tommy, who speaks from his grave. Blaming herself for Tommy's suicide, Annie believes that he did not trust her enough to talk to her about his feelings and his plans. In her soliloquy preceding this scene, she says, "We had something special. . . . It's all gone now. . . ."

TOMMY: I'm really sorry, Annie. (*She doesn't answer.*) Annie?

ANNIE: (*Totally ignoring* TOMMY) It was just not fair, do you hear me?

TOMMY: Annie, it wasn't you. Really.

ANNIE: I'll never know now if it was me. If I hurt you.

TOMMY: Oh, no. Annie, you were the best thing that ever happened to me. You were. Annie?

ANNIE: You used to tell me everything, I thought.

TOMMY: I did tell you everything. At least at first.

ANNIE: (*She gets up and walks around, clutching her flowers.*) And I always told you everything. There were no secrets between us. None.

TOMMY: I know.

ANNIE: If I was mad, you knew it.

TOMMY: (*Smiles*) I know.

ANNIE: Maybe I was a grouch at times . . .

TOMMY: Hey. Never.

ANNIE: (*To herself*) Yes. I was. I know I was. And we'd argue and fight. (*She smells the flowers.*) But we always made up, Tommy.

TOMMY: We sure did. I'll always remember that. One of my good memories.

ANNIE: So why? Can you tell me?

TOMMY: (*Gets up and follows her around, but she doesn't ever look at him. He tries to catch her eye, but can't.*) I can tell you this much . . . Annie? Can you hear me? It wasn't you.

ANNIE: I know it was me. It was always me.

TOMMY: (*Trying to catch her eye*) No. No. It wasn't! I loved you! I always loved you! I'll always love you.

ANNIE: You probably just got tired of my grouchiness.

TOMMY: No. Never. Hey, I was a grouch at times, myself. Remember?

ANNIE: But you were no angel, Tommy.

TOMMY: (*Sits on bench*) Tell me about it.

ANNIE: (*Covers her mouth for a second*) Oh, I'm sorry.

TOMMY: Hey. Stop apologizing. I'm not worth it.

ANNIE: See? Even now I hurt you. You never thought much about yourself, and when I called you names you must have really been hurt.

TOMMY: Yeah, I was—but I deserved it, Annie.

ANNIE: You'd always say, "But I deserved it, Annie." (*Pause as* TOMMY *nods*) I miss you, Tommy. Do you know that?

TOMMY: I do now. Yes, I do now.

ANNIE: No matter how much we fought or called each other names, I still miss you. And you didn't even say goodbye. People who love each other shouldn't do that.

TOMMY: I know.

ANNIE: You should have told me something was wrong. I'd never have left you. I loved you.

TOMMY: I was going to write a note, but . . . I couldn't think of what to say. What could I say? You know me? I was never much with words.

ANNIE: You were never good with words.

TOMMY: Hey. I could barely spell.

ANNIE: And your spelling. You spelled "Love" (*Spelling*) L-U-V.

TOMMY: She remembers.

ANNIE: How could I forget that? You were never good with words. You had other ways of showing me you loved me.

TOMMY: Now that is one thing I'll really miss.

ANNIE: Big macho man. You'd die if the guys knew how you used to pick me daisies at the lake and put them in my hair . . .

TOMMY: Annie, don't . . . (*he's in real pain.*)

ANNIE: Who'd buy me silly cards and mail them to me for no reason . . . but to . . .

TOMMY: Please don't, Annie . . .

ANNIE: For no reason, but because . . .

TOMMY: Don't.

ANNIE: Because you loved me.

TOMMY: (*It's as if he's been wounded*) I loved you, Annie! I did. Annie, please don't be sad.

ANNIE: Everyone keeps saying, "Annie, please don't be sad."

TOMMY: I'm not worth it, Annie.

ANNIE: "He's not worth it, Annie."

TOMMY: Annie . . . please . . . Annie.

ANNIE: Annie, Annie, Annie. What do they know? (*She sits beside him on the bench.*) What did anyone know? How can they possibly know how I feel? You broke my heart.

TOMMY: Annie, I didn't know.

ANNIE: Tommy . . .

TOMMY: Yes . . .

ANNIE: Why did you do this to me, Tommy? Can you tell me?

TOMMY: It had nothing to do with you! Can't you hear me?

ANNIE: I know it was me.

TOMMY: (*Screaming in pain*) NO! IT WAS NOT YOU!

ANNIE: Yes.

TOMMY: No, no. Can't you understand? It was not you, Annie. I love you.

ANNIE: He never really loved me.

TOMMY: (*In real pain*) What?

ANNIE: If you loved me, you'd have told me.

TOMMY: I did love you! And it had nothing to do with you. Nothing!

ANNIE: Whatever it was, it had something to do with me.

TOMMY: No.

ANNIE: Yes, I guess we're all partially to blame . . . That's what everyone says.

TOMMY: No.

ANNIE: I know it's true. I'll never forgive myself.

TOMMY: It's not your fault, Annie.

ANNIE: Yes. It had something to do with me.

TOMMY: No, no, no . . .

ANNIE: It had everything to do with us—

TOMMY: How can you say that?

ANNIE: —because we were friends. And friends help each other no matter what it is that is bothering them. That's what friends are for.

TOMMY: Annie, Im sorry. I should have told you.

ANNIE: Tommy, no matter what it was, I would have understood. You should have told me.

TOMMY: Annie, I'll tell you now. Can you hear me? Annie? Are you listening to me?

ANNIE: We always listened to each other. Always.

TOMMY: Always.

ANNIE: But now it's too late.

TOMMY: No.

ANNIE: Yes. too late. You're gone forever.

TOMMY: Annie, I'm right here. Beside you. Right on this bench. Can't you see me?

ANNIE: I'll never see you again.

TOMMY: Annie, look! I'm right here!

ANNIE: If I could only feel your arms around me.

TOMMY: (*He hugs her, but she feels nothing*) Annie, I love you!

ANNIE: (*She shivers.*) What was that icy chill?

TOMMY: Chill?

ANNIE: I must be getting a cold. (*She stands.*)

TOMMY: A chill? From me? I love you.

ANNIE: I'd tell you how much I loved you. but it's too late for that now. I'll never know why you did it, Tommy.

TOMMY: Annie, neither will I!

ANNIE: It was so sudden.

TOMMY: It was a dumb, stupid mistake. I was just so down over so many things. It seemed there was nothing left.

ANNIE: You could have gotten help. Everyone can.

TOMMY: I know that now.

ANNIE: It's too late now. I know you could have worked things out. Even this. Together we could have.

TOMMY: Yes.

ANNIE: I guess for as long as I live, I'll always blame myself for what happened.

TOMMY: Oh, no. Annie, I'll never be able to rest in peace if you think that.

ANNIE: (*Goes over to headstone*) Look at these weeds. (*She gets on her knees, puts flowers on ground and pulls weeds away little by little, revealing the headstone of TOMMY's grave. She picks up the flowers and lays them on the grave.*) These are for you, Tommy. Daisies.

TOMMY: Annie, I love you.

ANNIE: I'm sorry if I caused you any pain. And I'm sorry if I can't come to see you anymore . . .

TOMMY: What? No . . .

ANNIE: It's been a year now. A whole new summer is here. It's beautiful. I wish we could enjoy it together. I wish I could be with you, but my doctor says it's not healthy to dwell on the past. So, Tommy, I've come for the last time . . .

TOMMY: Oh, no . . . please, Annie, don't leave me.

ANNIE: I just had to come here one last time . . .

TOMMY: No . . .

ANNIE: I had to come just one more time just to say goodbye to you . . . my dear, sweet friend . . . Tommy. (*She stands.*)

TOMMY: Annie, no. Don't go. I love you! Don't go!

ANNIE: I have to go. Goodbye, Tommy. (*She exits.*)

TOMMY: Noooo . . . Annie, please don't leave me alone. Annie! (*Curtain falls as TOMMY puts his head in his hands.*)

Questions for Discussion

1. Speculate on why Tommy killed himself. Why do you think he did not tell Annie how he was feeling before he died?

2. What sort of person is Annie? Describe her feelings about Tommy's killing himself.

3. Why do you think Annie's doctor suggested she not visit Tommy's grave anymore? Do you agree that she shouldn't? Why?

4. Discounting the fact that the dead do not talk with the living, do you think Tommy is a realistic character? Why? Is Annie? Why?

5. From clues given in this scene and the stage directions, what sort of relationship do you think Annie and Tommy had when he was alive?

Zonia Loomis: 11
Reuben Scott: About 11
Length of scene: Six to seven minutes

Joe Turner's Come and Gone

August Wilson/ *U.S.A.*

The play begins when Herald Loomis and his 11-year-old daughter arrive at a Pittsburgh, Pennsylvania, boarding house. It is 1911, when African Americans—the children of slaves—are just beginning their great migration from the agrarian south to the industrial north. In setting the scene, Wilson says: "The sun falls out of heaven like a stone. The fires of the steel mill rage with a combined sense of industry and progress. Barges loaded with coal and iron ore trudge up the river to the mill towns that dot the Monongahela and return with fresh, hard, gleaming steel."

After spending years on a chain gang, during which time his daughter, Zonia, stayed with her grandmother, Loomis is looking for his wife. When Zonia asks where she is, her father tells her that "some man named Joe Turner did something to him once and that made her run away."

Shortly after arriving in Pittsburgh, Zonia meets Reuben, a boy who lives nearby. He tells her he had a friend who died. Reuben is keeping Eugene's pigeons. While Eugene himself kept pigeons, he sold some periodically to a "conjure man," a local man who practiced magic. Later, Eugene told Reuben that after he died, Reuben was to free the pigeons. He hasn't done so. He says he wants to keep them to remember his friend, and he also sells pigeons to the conjure man—whose name is Mr. Bynum. This scene takes place about a week and a half after Zonia has arrived in Pittsburgh.

(*It is early in the morning. The lights come up on* ZONIA *and* REUBEN *in the yard.*)

REUBEN: Something spooky going on around here. Last night Mr. Bynum was out in the yard singing and talking to the wind . . . and the wind it just be talking back to him. Did you hear it?

ZONIA: I heard it. I was scared to get up and look. I thought it was a storm.

REUBEN: That wasn't no storm. That was Mr. Bynum. First he say something . . . and the wind say it back to him.

ZONIA: I heard it. Was you scared? I was scared.

REUBEN: And then this morning . . . I seen Miss Mabel!

ZONIA: Who Miss Mabel?

REUBEN: Mr. Seth's mother. He got her picture hanging up in the house. She been dead.

ZONIA: How you seen her if she been dead?

REUBEN: Zonia . . . if I tell you something you promise you won't tell anybody?

ZONIA: I promise.

REUBEN: It was early this morning . . . I went out to the coop to feed the pigeons. I was down on the ground like this to open up the door to the coop . . . when all of a sudden I seen some feets in front of me. I looked up . . . and there was Miss Mabel standing there.

ZONIA: Reuben, you better stop telling that! You ain't seen nobody!

REUBEN: Naw, it's the truth. I swear! I seen her just like I see you. Look . . . you can see where she hit me with her cane.

ZONIA: Hit you? What she hit you for?

REUBEN: She say. "Didn't you promise Eugene something?" Then she hit me with her cane. She say, "Let them pigeons go." Then she hit me again. That's what made them marks.

ZONIA: Jeez man . . . get away from me. You done seen a haunt!

REUBEN: Shhh. You promised, Zonia!

ZONIA: You sure it wasn't Miss Bertha come over there and hit you with her hoe?

REUBEN: It wasn't no Miss Bertha. I told you it was Miss Mabel. She was standing right there by the coop. She had this light coming out of her and then she just melted away.

ZONIA: What she had on?

REUBEN: A white dress. Ain't even had no shoes or nothing. Just had on that white dress and them big hands . . . and that cane she hit me with.

ZONIA: How you reckon she knew about the pigeons? You reckon Eugene told her?

REUBEN: I don't know. I sure ain't asked her none. She say Eugene was waiting on them pigeons. Say he couldn't go back home till I let them go. I couldn't get the door to the coop open fast enough.

ZONIA: Maybe she an angel? From the way you say she look with that white dress. Maybe she an angel.

REUBEN: Mean as she was . . . how she gonna be an angel? She used to chase us out her yard and frown up and look evil all the time.

ZONIA: That don't mean she can't be no angel cause of how she looked and cause she wouldn't let no kids play in her yard. It go by if you got any spots on your heart and if you pray and go to church.

REUBEN: What about she hit me with her cane? An angel wouldn't hit me with her cane.

ZONIA: I don't know. She might. I still say she was an angel.

REUBEN: You reckon Eugene the one who sent Old Miss Mabel?

ZONIA: Why he send her? Why he don't come himself?

REUBEN: Figured if he send her maybe that'll make me listen. Cause she old.

ZONIA: What you think it feel like?

REUBEN: What?

ZONIA: Being dead.

REUBEN: Like being sleep only you don't know nothin' and can't move no more.

ZONIA: If Miss Mabel can come back . . . then maybe Eugene can come back too.

REUBEN: We can go down to the hideout like we used to! He could come back everyday! It be just like he ain't dead.

ZONIA: Maybe that ain't right for him to come back. Feel kinda funny to be playing games with a haunt.

REUBEN: Yeah . . . what if everybody came back. What if Miss Mabel came back just like she ain't dead. Where you and your daddy gonna sleep then?

ZONIA: Maybe they go back at night and don't need no place to sleep.

REUBEN: It still don't seem right. I'm sure gonna miss Eugene. He's the bestest friend anybody ever had.

ZONIA: My daddy say if you miss somebody too much it can kill you. Say he missed me till it liked to killed him.

REUBEN: What if your mama's already dead and all the time you looking for her?

ZONIA: Naw, she ain't dead. My daddy say he can smell her.

REUBEN: You can't smell nobody that ain't here. Maybe he smelling old Miss Bertha. Maybe Miss Bertha your mama?

ZONIA: Naw she ain't. My mama got long pretty hair and she five feet from the ground!

REUBEN: Your daddy say when you leaving? (ZONIA *doesn't respond*) Maybe you gonna stay in Mr. Seth's house and don't go looking for your mama no more.

ZONIA: He say we got to leave on Saturday.

REUBEN: Dag! You just only been here for a little while. Don't seem like nothing ever stay the same.

ZONIA: He say he got to find her. Find him a place in the world.

REUBEN: He could find him a place at Mr. Seth's house.

ZONIA: It don't look like we never gonna find her.

REUBEN: Maybe he find her by Saturday then you don't have to go.

ZONIA: I don't know.

REUBEN: You look like a spider.

ZONIA: I ain't no spider.

REUBEN: Got them long skinny arms and legs. You look like one of them Black Widows.

ZONIA: I ain't got no Black Widow nothing! My name is Zonia!

REUBEN: That's what I'm gonna call you . . . Spider.

ZONIA: You can call me that, but I don't have to answer.

REUBEN: You know what? I think maybe I be your husband when I grow up.

ZONIA: How you know?

REUBEN: I ask my grandpap how you know and he say when the moon falls into a girl's eyes that how you know.

ZONIA: Did it fall into my eyes?

REUBEN: Not that I can tell. Maybe I ain't old enough. Maybe you ain't old enough.

ZONIA: So there! I don't know why you telling me that lie!

REUBEN: That don't mean nothing cause I can't see it. I know it's there. Just the way you look at me sometimes look like the moon might have been in your eyes.

ZONIA: That don't mean nothing if you can't see it. You supposed to see it.

REUBEN: Shucks, I see it good enough for me. You ever let anybody kiss you?

ZONIA: Just my daddy. He kiss me on the cheek.

REUBEN: It's better on the lips. Can I kiss you on the lips?

ZONIA: I don't know.

REUBEN: It don't hurt or nothing. It feels good.

ZONIA: You ever kiss anybody before?

REUBEN: I had a cousin let me kiss her on the lips one time. Can I kiss you?

ZONIA: Okay. (REUBEN *kisses her and lays his head against her chest*) What you doing?

REUBEN: Listening. Your heart singing!

ZONIA: It is not.

REUBEN: Just beating like a drum. Let's kiss again. (*They kiss again*) Now you mine, Spider. You my girl, okay?

ZONIA: Okay.

REUBEN: When I get grown, I come looking for you.

ZONIA: Okay.

(*The lights fade.*)

Questions for Discussion

1. Why do you think Reuben says, after he has kissed Zonia, that she is now his? Is this believable? Explain.

2. What do you think life was like for newly arrived African Americans in Pittsburgh in 1911? Explain.

3. From the scene, what can you tell about Zonia and Reuben's feelings about Mr. Bynum? Is it logical they feel this way? Explain.

4. What do you think Zonia's father meant when he told her he could "smell" her mother, so he knows she is still alive?

5. What do you think the future would hold for young African Americans like Zonia and Reuben who lived at this time? Why?

Stanja: About 20 (female)
Mirko: Early 20s (male)
Length of scene: Two minutes and 45 seconds to three minutes and 15 seconds

Goat Song

Franz Werfel/*Austria*

Written in 1926, the play takes place at the close of the eighteenth century. In the following scene, Stanja—who is betrothed to Mirko—has just been dropped off by her parents, to stay with his family and get used to the farm.

Later in the play, it is discovered that a little stone building on the property houses Mirko's deformed and "beastlike" brother, who has been hidden away since birth. Eventually this mysterious character becomes the symbol for a group of peasants, led by a student (scholar) named Juvan, who overrun the property of wealthy landowners. The theme of *Goat Song* is that there are consequences for becoming too passionate about anything.

MIRKO: Your parents are gone now. Are you sad?

STANJA: No, I am not sad.

MIRKO: Then you don't love your parents?

STANJA: I love them.

MIRKO: Then you must be sad. Doesn't it hurt you when something is over? The axle creaks, the horses draw up, the whip. . . . And then, something is ended.

STANJA: I never ache for what is past.

MIRKO: Oh, I often do. I can lie in the meadow hour after hour longing for the games I played there on the grass.

STANJA: That is because you are a man.

(*Short pause*)

MIRKO: Do the house and the farm please you?

STANJA: Why shouldn't they? House, rooms, chimneys, stables, pigsties, and hencoops and dovecotes, same as everywhere.

MIRKO: And do I please you?

STANJA: Why shouldn't you please me?

MIRKO: Do you know, Stanja, I would have liked it better if you had cried before, when they left you. . . . (*Suddenly turns on her*) You! What if you've loved someone before! Tell me! Have you loved someone else?

STANJA (*Hesitatingly*): No.

MIRKO (*Slowly, his eyes closed*): I think, when we're married, I will beat you.

STANJA: That's what all husbands do.

MIRKO: Did you tell me the truth?

STANJA: No.

MIRKO: Ah! You did love another before me, before me . . .

STANJA: Did I love him? Just one, I dreamed of him in the night. He'd been our guest for an hour. He wore a scholar's cap on his head and a laced coat. He was a student.

MIRKO (*Presses her hand*): Did he speak to you? Did you see him again? Or dream of him?

STANJA: Never again.

MIRKO (*Lets her hand fall, brusquely*): A student? Ho! You want to show me you're a smart one.

STANJA (*Flushing*): That takes no showing.

MIRKO: Damn!

STANJA: You led me through the rooms and closets up to the attic. We looked at all the stalls, the cattle, the dairies, the storehouse, the threshing floors, wine presses, everything. But I have eyes . . .

MIRKO (*Excited, tries to embrace her*): Blue eyes, sharp, bad, sweet . . .

STANJA (*Thrusts him from her*): But mighty quick you slipped by that little house of stone, and by that rusty iron door. You wouldn't look, and pushed me away. (*Triumphant*) What does the smoking chimney of that big kennel mean? You light no fire for animals. That rising smoke is human . . . I have eyes!

MIRKO (*Stroking his forehead in helpless bewilderment*): I do not know, Stanja. Believe me, I do not know. Ever since I was a little child that was the forbidden place that we hurried by in fear, with downcast eyes. I dared not ask my mother or my father. I love my—father— not as you love yours. So I kept still and let my father bear the secret. I got used to it as a child and never gave it thought. But now! For twenty years, day after day, I have passed it—and always with my foreboding heart, yet never thinking of it. And now, all of a sudden, after so many years, I'm forced to think. . . . Yes, true enough! A fire's there each spring and winter. (*Seized by an obscure horror*) Stanja! I will not ask my father. I'll never ask.

STANJA: Now do you see who is the smart one? For twenty years you never thought or asked. But a woman comes to the house and asks you the first hour.

Questions for Discussion

1. Who do you think is more true to life, Stanja or Mirko? Explain.

2. Why do you suppose Stanja says she does not miss her parents? Keeping the setting of this play in mind, why do you think Mirko says he will beat her after they are married?

3. Why do you suppose Mirko has never investigated nor asked about the small building where smoke can be seen rising from the chimney?

4. What sort of married life do you think Stanja and Mirko would have? Why?

5. How would you interpret each character on stage? Which do you see as being more passionate in this scene?

The Merchant of Venice

William Shakespeare/*England*

At the beginning of the play, Bassanio has asked Antonio to lend him money so that he can romance Portia, a rich heiress. (Antonio, the merchant of the play's title, ends up borrowing the money from a moneylender—Shylock.) With the money, Bassanio sets out to win Portia's hand in marriage.

The problem is that her father's will has decreed that she shall marry the man who chooses the correct one of three chests or "caskets"—one of gold, one of silver, and one of lead. Two princes already have chosen wrong.

As the scene opens, there is a gathering and Bassanio is about to choose the casket he hopes is the right one. Portia has sensed their mutual attraction and apparently wants to help him choose, but she is forbidden to do so.

However, Portia orders that music be played and a song is sung while Bassanio makes his choice. It can be argued that the song helps him choose correctly because the song contends that "fancy" or love that begins "in the eyes" dies young. Portia seems to have found a way to encourage Bassanio to choose the lead casket.

When presenting the scene, the actor playing Portia can simply recite the song and the chorus's lines, or make up a tune to go with the words.

PORTIA:
  I pray you, tarry. Pause a day or two
  Before you hazard, for in choosing wrong
  I lose your company. Therefore forbear awhile.
  There's something tells me, but it is not love,
  I would not lose you; and you know yourself,
  Hate counsels not in such a quality.[1]
  But lest you should not understand me well—
  And yet a maiden hath no tongue but thought—[2]
  I would detain you here some month or two
  Before you venture for me. I could teach you
  How to choose right, but then I am forsworn.[3]
  So will I never be. So may you miss me.
  But if you do, you'll make me wish a sin,
  That I had been forsworn. Beshrew[4] your eyes,
  They have o'erlooked[5] me and divided me!
  One half of me is yours, the other half yours—
  Mine own, I would say; but if mine, then yours,
  And so all yours. O, these naughty[6] times
  Puts bars between the owners and their rights!
  And so, though yours, not yours.[7] Prove it so,
  Let Fortune go to hell for it, not I.
  I speak too long, but 'tis to peise[8] the time,
  To eke[9] it and to draw it out in length,
  To stay you from election.

BASSANIO: Let me choose,
  For as I am. I live upon the rack.[10]

---

[1] manner

[2] When a woman thinks, she has to speak.

[3] perjured

[4] Evil befall; meant humorously.

[5] bewitched

[6] wicked or worthless

[7] I am yours in my very being, but not yours in fact.

[8] piece out

[9] increase (eke out)

[10] An instrument of torture, used to stretch out the body until the joints separated.

PORTIA:
Upon the rack, Bassanio? Then confess
What treason there is mingled with your love.[11]

BASSANIO:
None but that ugly treason of mistrust,
Which makes me fear th' enjoying of my love.
There may as well be amity and life
'Tween snow and fire, as treason and my love.

PORTIA:
Ay, but I fear you speak upon the rack
Where men enforcèd[12] do speak anything.

BASSANIO:
Promise me life and I'll confess the truth.

PORTIA:
Well then, confess and live.

BASSANIO: Confess and love
Had been the very sum of my confession.
O happy torment when my torturer
Doth teach me answers for deliverance!
But let me to my fortune and the caskets.

PORTIA:
Away then! I am locked in one of them;
If you do love me, you will find me out.
Nerissa and the rest, stand all aloof.
Let music sound while he doth make his choice,
Then if he lose he makes a swanlike[13] end,
Fading in music. That the comparison
May stand more proper, my eye shall be the stream
And wat'ry deathbed for him. He may win
And what is music then? Then music is
Even as the flourish[14] when true subjects bow
To a new-crowned monarch; such it is
As are those dulcet sounds in break of day
That creep into the dreaming bridegroom's ear

---

[11] The rack was used to make people confess to treason.

[12] under torture

[13] It was believed that a swan sang only once—just before its death.

[14] fanfare

And summon him to marriage. Now he goes
With no less presence but with much more love
Than young Alcides[15] when he did redeem
The virgin tribute[16] paid by howling Troy
To the sea monster. I stand for sacrifice;
The rest aloof are the Dardanian[17] wives
With bleared visages[18] come forth to view
The issue[19] of th' exploit. Go, Hercules!
Live thou, I live. With much, much more dismay
I view the fight than thou that mak'st the fray.

(*A song [sung as] the whilst* BASSANIO *comments on the caskets to himself.*)

> *Tell me where is fancy[20] bred,*
> *Or in the heart or in the head?*
> *How begot, how nourishèd?*

CHORUS: *Reply, reply.*

> *It is engend'red in the eyes,*
> *With gazing fed, and fancy dies*
> *In the cradle where it lies*
> *Let us all ring fancy's knell.[21]*
> *I'll begin it—Ding, dong, bell.*

CHORUS: *Ding, dong, bell.*

BASSANIO:
So may the outward shows be least themselves;
The world is still deceived with ornament:
In law, what plea so tainted and corrupt
But being seasoned[22] with a gracious voice
Obscures the show of evil? In religion,

---

[15] Alcides is another name for Hercules, who rescued Hesione, not out of love, but for the reward of a team of horses.

[16] Unless a virgin was offered for the monster to devour, it would continue to threaten Troy.

[17] Trojan

[18] weeping eyes

[19] result

[20] love

[21] the tolling of a bell, for a funeral

[22] as bad food is hidden by a strong sauce

What damned error but some sober brow
Will bless it and approved[23] it with a text,
Hiding the grossness with fair ornament?
There is no vice so simple but assumes
Some mark of virtue on his outward parts.
How many cowards, whose hearts are all as false[24]
As stairs of sand, wear yet upon their chins
The beards of Hercules and frowning Mars,
Who, inward search, have livers white as milk![25]
And these assume but valor's excrement[26]
To render them redoubted.[27] Look on beauty.
And you shall see 'tis purchased by the weight,[28]
Which therein works a miracle in nature,
Making them lightest[29] that wear most of it.
So are those crispèd snaky[30] golden locks,
Which maketh such wanton gambols with the wind
Upon supposèd fairness, often known
To be the dowry of a second head,
The skull that bred them in the sepulcher.[31]
Thus ornament is but the guilèd[32] shore
To a most dangerous sea, the beauteous scarf
Veiling an Indian beauty; in a word,
The seeming truth which cunning times put on
To entrap the wisest. Therefore, thou gaudy gold,
Hard food for Midas, I will none of thee;
Nor none of thee, thou pale and common drudge[33]
'Tween man and man. But thou, thou meager lead
Which rather threaten'st than dost promise aught,

---

[23] confirm with a biblical text

[24] completely bad

[25] The liver was believed to be the seat of passion. When the blood was cold, the liver was supposed to be pale, a sign of cowardice. Today we still use the term *lily-livered*.

[26] Refers to hair or nails; here it refers to a fine, manly beard.

[27] dreaded

[28] It is cosmetic and bought at so much per ounce.

[29] Most unchaste; this is a pun on the word *light* as meaning little.

[30] Curled and long and sinuous, alluding to a snake's poison and deceit.

[31] Wig made from the hair of a dead person.

[32] treacherous

[33] Refers to silver, used for common trade and so unglamorous.

Thy paleness moves me more than eloquence;
And here choose I. Joy be the consequence!

PORTIA: (*Aside*)
How all the other passions fleet to air,
As doubtful thoughts, and rash-embraced despair,
And shuddering fear, and green-eyed jealousy!
O love, be moderate, allay thy ecstasy,
In measure rain thy joy, scant[34] this excess!
I feel too much thy blessing. Make it less,
For fear I surfeit.[35]

BASSANIO: (*Opening the leaden casket*)
                              What find I here?
Fair Portia's counterfeit![36] What demigod
Hath come so near creation? Move these eyes?
Or whether, riding on the balls of mine,[37]
Seem they in motion? Here are severed[38] lips,
Parted with sugar breath; so sweet a bar[39]
Should sunder such sweet friends. Here in her hairs
The painter plays the spider, and hath woven
A golden mesh t' entrap the hearts of men
Faster[40] than gnats in cobwebs. But her eyes—
How could he see to do them? Having made one,
Methinks it should have power to steal both his
And leave itself unfurnished.[41] Yet look how far
The substance[42] of my praise doth wrong this shadow[43]
In underprizing it, so far this shadow
Doth limp behind the substance. Here's the scroll,
The continent[44] and summary of my fortune.

---

[34] lessen

[35] fall ill from excess

[36] portrait

[37] eyeballs

[38] separated

[39] Portia's breath

[40] more secure

[41] without a companion

[42] Portia herself

[43] painting

[44] container

(*Reads*)   *You that choose not by the view*
          Chance as fair, and choose as true.
          Since this fortune falls to you,
          Be content and seek no new.
          If you be well pleased with this
          And hold your fortune for your bliss,
          Turn you where your lady is,
          And claim her with a loving kiss.

A gentle[45] scroll. Fair lady, by your leave,
I come by note[46] to give and to receive,
Like one of two contending in a prize[47]
That thinks he hath done well in people's eyes,
Hearing applause and universal shout,
Giddy in spirit, still gazing in a doubt
Whether those peals of praise be his or no,
So, thrice-fair lady, stand I even so,
As doubtful whether what I see be true
Until confirmed, signed, ratified by you.

PORTIA:
You see me, Lord Bassanio, where I stand,
Such as I am. Though for myself alone
I would not be ambitious in my wish
To wish myself much better, yet for you
I would be trebled twenty times myself,
A thousand times more fair, ten thousand times more rich,
That only to stand high in your account[48]
I might in virtues, beauties, livings,[49] friends,
Exceed account. But the full sum of me
Is sum of something—which, to term in gross,
Is an unlessoned girl, unschooled, unpracticed;
Happy in this, she is not yet so old
But she may learn; happier than this,
She is not bred so dull but she can learn;
Happiest of all, is that her gentle spirit
Commits itself to yours to be directed

---

[45] courteous

[46] according to what was said

[47] prize fight

[48] esteem/financial reckoning

[49] possessions

As from her lord, her governor, her king.
Myself, and what is mine, to you and yours
Is now converted.[50] But now I was the lord
Of this fair mansion, master of my servants,
Queen o'er myself; and even now, but now,
This house, these servants and this same myself
Are yours—my lord's!—I give them with this ring,
Which when you part from, lose or give away,
Let it presage[51] the ruin of your love
And be my vantage to exclaim[52] on you.

BASSANIO:
Madam, you have bereft me of all words,
Only my blood speaks to you in my veins
And there is such confusion in my powers
As after some oration fairly spoke
By a beloved prince there doth appear
Among the buzzing pleasèd multitude,
Where every something being blent together
Turns to a wild of nothing save of joy
Expressed and not expressed. But when this ring
Parts from this finger, then parts life from hence—
O then be bold to say Bassanio's dead!

---

[50] transformed

[51] foretell

[52] opportunity to accuse you

Questions for Discussion

1. Why do you suppose the father left a stipulation in his will that his daughter's suitors had to choose the proper casket in order to marry her?

2. Why does Portia ask Bassanio (in the speech that opens this scene) to "pause a day or two before you hazard" to choose a casket?

3. Bassanio says he lives on the rack, that is, in torture, because he wants the choosing finished. Why then do you think Portia asked him what treason was mixed with his love? Considering the circumstances, is it reasonable she would do this? Why?

4. What logic, if any, does Bassanio follow in choosing the correct casket? What emotions does he express upon opening the right casket? Point out the lines of dialogue that show this.

5. In everyday language, how does Portia respond after Bassanio has chosen the casket with her portrait in it?

Scenes for
Two Females

Christine: 20
Lea: Late teens
Length of scene: Two minutes and 45 seconds
to three minutes and 15 seconds

My Sister in This House

Wendy Kesselman/ *U.S.A.*

This play tells the story of two sisters who work as maids in a house in Le Mans, France, in 1933. It is based on a true incident, which Kesselman says obsessed her until the play finally was finished and produced.

Christine and Lea (According to the author, this should be pronounced Léa.) grew up in a series of convents because their mother, also a maid, was not able to care for them. Because of this, the two girls came to rely on each other. As soon as Christine was old enough to work, however, their mother insisted on placing her as a maid.

As this scene begins, Lea is now of age and has been placed as a maid—in the same household as Christine.

CHRISTINE: (*Softly*) What is it, Lea? Another letter from Maman? (LEA *looks away. Gently.*) Well, go on. Read it. There's no reason to stop just because I came into the room. (*She takes off her long apron and folds it neatly.*)

LEA: I'll read it later.

CHRISTINE: You won't have time later. You're exhausted by ten. Read it now. (LEA *looks at her. Smiling.*) Why don't you read it out lͬ ͺuͬ

LEA: (*Nervously*) Do you really want me to?

CHRISTINE: I wouldn't say it otherwise. Would I?

LEA: (*Unfolding the letter, begins to read*) "Lea, my pet, my little dove. I know I'll see you Sunday as usual, but I miss you. Little Lea. You'll always be little."

CHRISTINE: Go on.

LEA: (*Continuing*) "Don't forget to bring me the money. You forgot last week."

CHRISTINE: Poor Maman.

LEA: Christine—Maman just—

CHRISTINE: Maman just what? (*Changing. Gentle.*) Go ahead. Keep reading.

LEA: (*Going on with the letter*) "You can't wear your hair that way anymore, Lea. Like a child. All that long hair." (*She stops*)

CHRISTINE: Well? Don't leave anything out.

LEA: (*Going on*) "Next Sunday, when you come, I'll fix it for you. It'll be better that way. Like Christine's. Won't fall in the soup." (LEA *looks up, laughing.* CHRISTINE *doesn't smile.*) (*Going back to the letter. Quickly.*) "Or get Christine to fix it for you. But—" (*She stops*)

CHRISTINE: But what?

LEA: "Tell her to be gentle."

CHRISTINE: (*Snatching the letter from* LEA) I'm never going back.

LEA: Christine.

CHRISTINE: (*Folding the letter up very small*) You can go if you want to.

LEA: You know I wouldn't without you.

CHRISTINE: But you still care for her. She loves you.

LEA: But Christine, Christine. Maman loves you too. She's just . . .

CHRISTINE: What?

LEA: . . . scared of you.

CHRISTINE: Scared of me? (*Giving the tiny folded up letter back to* LEA) You never stick up for me. But that's right. Defend her. Take her part. Like you always do. (*Moving away*) Once she said that just to look at me made her sick. She couldn't even keep me after the first year. She hated when I cried.

Lea: Christine.

CHRISTINE: At Saint Mary of the Fields, I used to escape. Once a month. No one in this town would have brought me back—you know what they call it here. But your Maman—our Maman—she brought me back every time. In the end all I wanted was to be a nun. A nun! (*She smiles*) That's all I wanted. But then of course she took me out. She hadn't expected that. That was against all her plans. I had to work. I had to make money. And she kept all of it. She placed me—and each time I got used to it, she took me out again. Sometimes I'd run away. I ran back to the Sisters. They wanted to keep me. It was Maman, our beloved precious Maman, who would come and drag me out again.

LEA: Don't be angry with me.

CHRISTINE: I'm not angry with you.

LEA: Your face. It looks so—

CHRISTINE: (*Cutting in*) What? What's the matter with my face?

LEA: It just looked . . . Your face is beautiful. There's nothing wrong with your face.

CHRISTINE: No? (*She takes the hairbrush*) I'll fix it for you. Just like she said. I'll fix it. (*Tenderly starting to brush* LEA's *hair. Longingly.*) If we didn't go back we could have all out Sundays together, just to ourselves. We could walk, we could go to the station and watch the trains come in. We could sit in the square, we could—But no—you wouldn't want that, would you? You want to go back. Don't you? (*Pleading*) Don't you, Lea? (LEA *is silent* CHRISTINE *changes, violently brushes* LEA's *hair.*) Of course you do. (*Roughly, she twists* LEA's *hair into two buns on either side of her face.*) There. Like this. That's what she meant. (*Pulling* LEA *over to the mirror above the sink. Raging.*) Look. How do you like it?

LEA: (*Tearing out her hair and sobbing*) I hate it. (*She grabs the brush from* CHRISTINE *and tries to fix her own hair, putting it back the way*

it was. She does this clumsily, jerkily—too upset to get it right. CHRIS-
TINE *watches her in silence, suddenly overwhelmed at what she has
done.*)

CHRISTINE: I'm a monster—aren't I? Just like she says.

LEA: You're not a monster. (*She stops fixing her hair.*)

CHRISTINE: Here. Let me. (*Cautiously, she reaches for the brush.* LEA
hesitates, turns away.) I'll do it for you. (LEA *still hesitates*) Let me do
it—please. (LEA *is silent*) Please. (*Tentatively,* LEA *holds out the brush.*
CHRISTINE *takes it from her gently. Softly, slowly, she starts brushing*
LEA's *hair.*) What did you mean when you said my face was
beautiful?

LEA: What I said.

CHRISTINE: What's beautiful about it? Tell me one thing.

LEA: (*Looking up at her*) Your eyes.

Questions for Discussion

1. Why do you suppose Lea still wants to see her mother and Chris-
    tine doesn't?

2. Why do you think Christine is trying to influence Lea to stay with
    her on Sundays?

3. Why does Lea hesitate in reading the letter aloud to Christine?
    What are her feelings as she reads? What are Christine's feelings?

4. What sort of feelings do you think Christine has for Lea? Explain.
    What sort of feelings does Lea have for Christine? What makes you
    think so?

5. Do you think the sisters should continue to see their mother? Why?

Antigone: Probably about 18 or 20
Ismene: Probably early 20s
Length of scene: Five minutes and 45 seconds
to six minutes and 45 seconds

Antigone

Jean Anouilh/*France*

This is a modern version of an ancient Greek play, written in about 441 B.C. by Sophocles. Anouilh's play, written in 1944, closely follows the original plot. After the death of Antigone's father, Oedipus, king of Thebes, his two sons Eteocles and Polynices struggle for power—each killing one another in combat. Oedipus' brother-in-law Creon, who is now king, has ordered that Polynices not be buried but instead be left to rot. His sister Antigone defies Creon's order.

The central issue of this version is the meaning of life and the impossibility of maintaining purity in a world that demands compromise.

This scene occurs early in the play. Ismene does not know it, but her sister already has buried Polynices.

Just as in the original version, Antigone is put to death, and her fiancé, Haemon—Creon's son—commits suicide.

When practicing this scene, you can skip the one line the nurse has.

ISMENE: Aren't you well?

ANTIGONE: Of course I am. Just a little tired. I got up too early. (*She relaxes, suddenly tired.*)

ISMENE: I couldn't sleep, either.

ANTIGONE: Ismene, you ought not to go without your beauty sleep.

ISMENE: Don't make fun of me.

ANTIGONE: I'm not, Ismene, truly. This particular morning, seeing how beautiful you are makes everything easier for me. Wasn't I a miserable little beast when we were small? I used to fling mud at you, and put worms down your neck. I remember tying you to a tree and cutting off your hair. Your beautiful hair! How easy it must be never to be unreasonable with all that smooth silken hair so beautifully set round your head.

ISMENE: (*Abruptly*) Why do you insist upon talking about other things?

Antigone: (*Gently*) I'm not talking about other things.

ISMENE: Antigone, I've thought about it a lot.

ANTIGONE: Have you?

ISMENE: I thought about it all night long. Antigone, you're mad.

ANTIGONE: Am I?

ISMENE: We cannot do it.

ANTIGONE: Why not?

ISMENE: Creon will have us put to death.

ANTIGONE: Of course he will. That's what he's here for. He will do what he has to do, and we will do what we have to do. He is bound to put us to death. We are bound to go out and bury our brother. That's the way it is. What do you think we can do to change it?

ISMENE: (*Releases* ANTIGONE's *hand; draws back a step*) I don't want to die.

ANTIGONE: I'd prefer not to die, myself.

ISMENE: Listen to me, Antigone. I thought about it all night. I'm older than you are. I always think things over and you don't. You are impulsive. You get a notion in your head and you jump up and do the thing straight off. And if it's silly, well, so much the worse for you. Whereas, I think things out.

ANTIGONE: Sometimes it is better not to think too much.

ISMENE: I don't agree with you! Oh, I know it's horrible. And I pity Polynices just as much as you do. But all the same, I sort of see what Uncle Creon means.

ANTIGONE: I don't want to "sort of see" anything.

ISMENE: Uncle Creon is the king. He has to set an example!

Antigone: But I am not the king; and I don't have to set people examples. Little Antigone gets a notion in her head—the nasty brat, the wilful, wicked girl; and they put her in a corner all day, or they lock her up in the cellar. And she deserves it. She shouldn't have disobeyed!

ISMENE: There you go, frowning, glowering, wanting your own stubborn way in everything. Listen to me. I'm right oftener than you are.

ANTIGONE: I don't want to be right!

ISMENE: At least you can try to understand.

ANTIGONE: Understand! The first word I ever heard out of any of you was "understand." Why don't I "understand" that I must not play with water—cold, black, beautiful flowing water—because I'd spill it on the palace tiles. Or with earth, because earth dirties a little girl's frock. Why didn't I "understand" that nice children don't eat out of every dish at once; or give everything in their pockets to beggars; or run in the wind so fast that they fall down; or ask for a drink when they're perspiring; or want to go swimming when it's either too early or too late, merely because they happen to feel like swimming. Understand! I don't want to understand. There'll be time enough to understand when I'm old . . . if I ever *am* old. But not now.

ISMENE: He is stronger than we are, Antigone. He is the king. And the whole city is with him. Thousands and thousands of them, swarming through all the streets of Thebes.

Antigone: I am not listening to you.

ISMENE: His mob will come running, howling as it runs. A thousand arms will seize our arms. A thousand breaths will breathe into our faces. Like one single pair of eyes, a thousand eyes will stare at us. We'll be driven in a tumbrel through their hatred, through the smell of them and their cruel, roaring laughter. We'll be dragged to the scaffold for torture, surrounded by guards with their idiot faces all bloated, their animal hands clean-washed for the sacrifice, their beefy eyes squinting as they stare at us. And we'll know that no shrieking and no begging will make them understand that we want to live, for they are like slaves who do exactly as they've been told, without caring about right or wrong. And we shall suffer, we shall feel pain rising in us until it becomes so unbearable that we *know* it must stop. But it won't stop, it will go on rising and rising, like a screaming voice. Oh, I can't, I can't, Antigone! (*A pause*)

ANTIGONE: How well you have thought it all out.

ISMENE: I thought of it all night long. Didn't you?

ANTIGONE: Oh, yes.

ISMENE: I'm an awful coward, Antigone.

ANTIGONE: So am I. But what has that got to do with it?

ISMENE: But, Antigone! Don't you want to go on living?

ANTIGONE: Go on living! Who was it that was always the first out of bed because she loved the touch of the cold morning air on her bare skin? Who was always the last to bed because nothing less than infinite weariness could wean her from the lingering night? Who wept when she was little because there were too many grasses in the meadow, too many creatures in the field, for her to know and touch them all?

ISMENE: (*Clasps* ANTIGONE's *hands, in a sudden rush of tenderness*) Darling little sister!

ANTIGONE: (*Repulsing her*) No! For heaven's sake! Don't paw me! And don't let us start sniveling! You say you've thought it all out. The howling mob—the torture—the fear of death . . . they've made up your mind for you. Is that it?

ISMENE: Yes.

ANTIGONE: All right. They're as good excuses as any.

ISMENE: Antigone, be sensible. It's all very well for men to believe in ideas and die for them. But you are a girl!

ANTIGONE: Don't I know I'm a girl? Haven't I spent my life cursing the fact that I was a girl?

ISMENE: (*With spirit*) Antigone! You have everything in the world to make you happy. All you have to do is reach out for it. You are going to be married; you are young; you are beautiful—

ANTIGONE: I am not beautiful.

ISMENE: Yes, you are! Not the way other girls are. But it's always you that the little boys turn to look back at when they pass us in the street. And when you go by, the little girls stop talking. They stare and stare at you, until we've turned a corner.

ANTIGONE: (*A faint smile*) "Little boys—little girls."

ISMENE: (*Challengingly*) And what about Haemon?

ANTIGONE: I shall see Haemon this morning. I'll take care of Haemon. You always said I was mad; and it didn't matter how little I was or what I wanted to do. Go back to bed now, Ismene. The sun is coming up, and as you see, there is nothing I can do today. Our brother Polynices is as well guarded as if he had won the war and were sitting on his throne. Go along. You are pale with weariness.

ISMENE: What are you going to do?

NURSE: (*Calls from offstage*) Come along, my dove. Come to breakfast.

ANTIGONE: I don't feel like going to bed. However, if you like, I'll promise not to leave the house till you wake up. Nurse is getting me breakfast. Go and get some sleep. The sun is just up. Look at you: You can't keep your eyes open. Go.

ISMENE: And you will listen to reason, won't you? You'll let me talk to you about this again? Promise?

ANTIGONE: I promise. I'll let you talk. I'll let all of you talk. Go to bed, now. (ISMENE *goes to arch and exits.*) Poor Ismene!

Questions for Discussion

1. Can you put yourself in Antigone's place and imagine what it would be like for someone to declare that you could not bury your dead brother? How would you feel about this? What do you think you would do?

2. Why do you think Antigone wants to bury her brother, while Ismene argues that the two of them should follow their uncle's orders?

3. Why do you suppose Antigone says she does not want to "understand"?

4. How do you think the two sisters feel about each other? Explain.

5. Near the beginning of the scene, Ismene says that Antigone is mad or insane. Why does she say this? Is the accusation justified? Explain.

Olivia: 18 to 20
Viola: 18 to 20
Length of scene: Three minutes and 30 seconds to four minutes

Twelfth Night

William Shakespeare/*England*

Orsino, the Duke of Illyria, is blindly in love with the Countess Olivia. To plead his cause, he sends his page Cesario, who really is Viola, a shipwrecked gentlewoman in disguise. To complicate matters, she herself is in love with Orsino. Olivia refuses to pay any attention to the duke. Yet she falls in love with Orsino's page, Viola.

In the scene that follows, Viola, disguised as Cesario, again has asked to meet with Olivia because she realized that in their first meeting Olivia had been charmed by the young man she is pretending to be. She undertakes this second visit, perhaps hoping for a total rejection of the duke whom she would be free to pursue, or maybe only to have the situation resolved for better or worse.

OLIVIA: Let the garden door be shut and leave me
to my hearing. Give me your hand, sir

VIOLA:
My duty, madam, and most humble service.

OLIVIA:
What is your name?

VIOLA:
Cesario is your servant's name, fair princess.

OLIVIA:
My servant, sir? 'Twas never merry wold
Since lowly feigning[1] was called compliment.
Y' are servant to the Count Orsino, youth.

VIOLA:
And he is yours, and his must needs be yours:
Your servant's servant is your servant, madam.

OLIVIA:
For him, I think not on him: for his thoughts,
Would they were blanks rather than filled with me.

VIOLA:
Madam, I come to whet your gentle thoughts
On his behalf.

OLIVIA: O by your leave, I pray you:
I bade you never speak again of him,
But would you undertake another suit,
I had rather hear you to solicit that
Than music from the spheres.[2]

VIOLA: Dear lady—

OLIVIA:
Give me leave, I beseech you. I did send,
After the last enchantment you did here,
A ring in chase of you. So did I abuse[3]
Myself, my servant and, I fear me, you.
Under your hard construction[4] must I sit,

---

[1] humble pretense

[2] Celestial harmony, supposedly caused by the movement of the planets and stars.

[3] wrong

[4] interpretation

To force that on you in a shameful cunning
Which you knew none of yours. What might you think?
Have you not set mine honor at the stake
And baited it with all th' unmuzzled thoughts[5]
That tyrannous heart can think? To one of your receiving[6]
Enough is shown: a cypress,[7] not a bosom,
Hides my heart. So let me hear you speak.

VIOLA:
I pity you.

OLIVIA: That's a degree to love.

VIOLA:
No, not a grize,[8] for 'tis a vulgar proof[9]
That very oft we pity enemies.

OLIVIA:
Why then methinks 'tis time to smile again.
O world, how apt the poor are to be proud:
If one should be a prey, how much the better
To fall before the lion than the wolf. (*Clock strikes.*)
The clock upbraids me with the waste of time.
Be not afraid, good youth: I will not have you.
And yet, when wit and youth is come to harvest,[10]
Your wife is like to reap a proper[11] man.
There lies your way, due west.

VIOLA: Then westward ho![12]
Grace and good disposition[13] attend your ladyship.
You'll nothing, madam, to my lord by me?

OLIVIA:
Stay.
I prithee tell me what thou think'st of me.

---

[5] like a bear being bated by dogs at a stake (a sport during Elizabethan times)

[6] sensitivity

[7] a mourning veil

[8] step

[9] common experience

[10] when you are mature

[11] fine

[12] the cry of London watermen ready to row up the Thames

[13] peace of mind

VIOLA:
That you do think you are not what you are.

OLIVIA:
If I think so, I think the same of you.[14]

VIOLA:
Then think you right: I am not what I am.

OLIVIA:
I would you were are I would have you be.

VIOLA:
Would it be better, madam, than I am?
I wish it might, for now I am your fool.[15]

OLIVIA:
O what a deal of scorn looks beautiful
In the contempt and anger of his lip!
A murd'rous guilt shows not itself more soon
Than love that would seem hid: love's night is noon.[16]
Cesario, by the roses of the spring,
By maidhood,[17] honor, truth, and everything,
I love thee so that, maugre[18] all thy pride,
Do not extort thy reasons can my passion hide.
Nor wit nor reason from this clause,
For that I woo, thou therefore hast no cause,
But rather reason thus with reason fetter,
Love sought is good, but given unsought is better.[19]

VIOLA:
By innocence I swear and by my youth,
I have one heart, one bosom and one truth,[20]
And that no woman has, nor never none
Shall mistress be of it, save I alone.

---

[14] I likewise, think you are the lord you are not.

[15] You are making a fool of me.

[16] Love is clearly seen even when hidden.

[17] virginity

[18] in spite of

[19] Do not argue with yourself that because I, a woman, am the wooer, that therefore you have no reason to love me in return; rather, refute that argument in this way—it is good for a man to receive the love of a woman, but better yet to receive it without asking.

[20] one love, one affection and one devotion

And so adieu, good madam. Never more
Will I my master's tears to you deplore.

OLIVIA:
Yet come again, for thou perhaps mayst move
That heart which now abhors to like his love. *Exeunt.*

Questions for Discussion

1. Do you find the circumstances of the scene plausible or believable? Why?

2. In a number of his plays, Shakespeare relied on mistaken identities. Why do you suppose he did this?

3. Do you think love at first sight is possible? Explain.

4. At one point Olivia says to Viola, "I prithee tell me what thou think'st of me." What do you think Viola means when she responds with, "That you do think you are not what you are"?

5. What feelings would you try to communicate to an audience if you were playing the role of Viola? Keep in mind that probably there are some feelings Viola wants to hide from Olivia, but which she must communicate to an audience.

Lupe: 12
Leticia: 17
Length of scene: Two minutes and 15 seconds
to two minutes and 45 seconds

Shadow of a Man

Cherrie Moraga/ *U.S.A.*

The play was produced first by the Brava! For Women in the Arts and the Eureka Theatre Company in San Francisco in November of 1990. The title is symbolic of the constant and heavy presence of men in the lives of the female characters. In the play this is suggested by fathers and sons, as well as by the priest and even God the Father.

The setting of the play is the home of the Rodriquezes, a Mexican American family living in Los Angeles. The playwright states: "The play opens on the interior of the house in the places chiefly inhabited by mothers and daughters. The kitchen is the central feature with the bathroon at stage right, and the daughters' bedroom at stage left." The action occurs in Spring 1969.

As this scene opens, much of the dialogue between the two sisters concerns Rigo, the son of the family, who is getting married to a "gringa," a non-Hispanic woman. Manuel, their father, is sitting on the porch in this scene. He is suffering what is certainly angina, pains caused by a heart problem. He also is upset that his son Rigo will no longer allow Manuel to hug him.

The next morning. LETICIA *and* LUPE *are in the bathroom, in their bathrobes.* LETICIA *is standing in front of the mirror fixing her hair, while* LUPE *polishes a pair of white dress shoes.* MANUEL *sits on the porch, drinking a beer, a six pack next to him. It is cloudy. Lucha Villa's "Que me lleva el tren"[1] is playing on the radio.*

LUPE: I liked Teresa better.

LETICIA: I liked Teresa, too, but Rigo though he was too good for a Chicana,[2] so he's gonna marry a gringa.

LUPE: Well, he mus' love Karen.

LETICIA: Right.

LUPE: Doesn't he?

LETICIA: (*Referring to her hair*) C'mere, Lupe. Help me.

LUPE: Well, does he?

LETICIA: Does he what?

LUPE: Love her. Does he love Karen?

LETICIA: Who knows what he feels, man. Jus' forget it. Do you hear me? Don't think about him no more. He's gone. In a couple of hours he'll be married and that's it. We'll never see him again. (*Referring to her hairdo*) Lupe, hand me the Dippity Do. (LUPE *gets up, gives her the styling gel.* LETICIA *begins applying it to her bangs.* LUPE *moves in front of* LETICIA *to face the mirror. She stretches open her eyelids with her fingers.*) Lupe, get out of the way.

LUPE: You can see yourself in there . . . in the darkest part.

LETICIA: What? (LUPE *leans into the mirror for a closer look.*)

LUPE: Two little faces, one in each eye. It's like you got other people living inside you. Maybe you're not really you. Maybe they're the real you and the big you is just a dream you.

LETICIA: I swear you give me the creeps when you talk about this stuff. You're gonna make yourself nuts.

---

[1] "Catching the Train," a Spanish song

[2] a Mexican-American woman

LUPE: But I'm not kidding. I mean, how d'you know? How do you really know what's regular life and what's a sueño?[3]

LETICIA: You're talking to me aren't you? That's no dream. How many fingers do you see?

LUPE: Five.

LETICIA: Right! (*Grabs her face*) Five fingers around your fat little face. You feel this?

LUPE: Yeah. Yeah.

LETICIA: Thats what's real, 'manita.[4] What you can see, taste, and touch . . . that's real.

LUPE: I still say, you can't know for sure.

LETICIA: Say something else. You're boring me. (LUPE *sits. Puts her shoes on.*)

LUPE: I went over to Cholo Park yesterday.

LETICIA: You better not tell Mom. Some chick jus' got her lonche[5] down there the other day. They found her naked, man, all chopped up.

LUPE: Ooooh. Shaddup.

LETICIA: Well, it's true. What were you doing down there?

LUPE: Nut'ing. Jus' hanging out with Frances and her brother, Nacho.

LETICIA: God, I hate that huevón. Stupid cholo[6]. . . he jus' hangs out with you guys cuz nobody his own age will have anything to do with him. (*Beat.*) So what were you guys up to?

LUPE: (*Humming.*) Nut'ing.

LETICIA: C'mon. Fess up! Out with it!

LUPE: Nut'ing. The boys were jus' throwing cats.

LETICIA: What?

LUPE: They was throwing cats off the hill.

LETICIA: What d'yuh mean?

---

[3] (Spanish) dream

[4] (Sp.) "sis"

[5] (Sp.) lunch; a slang expression

[6] (Sp.) derogatory words

LUPE: Well, they stand up there, grab the gatos by the colas[7] and swing 'em above their heads and let 'em go. Ay, they let out such a grito![8] It's horrible! It sounds like a baby being killed!

Questions for Discusssion

1. Why do you suppose Lupe feels that she cannot tell the difference between dreaming and being awake?

2. How does Leticia feel about Rigo marrying a "gringa"? Cite lines from the scene to back up your interpretations.

3. Why do you think the playwright brought in the part about throwing the cats down the hill? Why do you think Lupe watched this?

4. In what ways do you see Lupe's and Leticia's lives being influenced by males? How do you suppose they feel about it?

5. Why do you think Lupe goes to the park when it is such a dangerous place?

---

[7] (Sp.) cats [by the] tails

[8] (Sp.) scream

Peggy: 14
Trish: 14
Length of scene: Two minutes and 30 seconds
to three minutes

Album

David Rimmer/ *U.S.A.*

The play, which takes place from October 1963 to June 1967, follows the maturation process of four teenagers: two girls and two boys. All are fourteen when the play begins, eighteen when it ends. Peggy is the school beauty, and Trish is her plain-looking best friend.

In this scene, which opens the play, the four of them have been playing strip poker. The stage directions state, "Trish is terrified, Peggy supremely confident. Boo loses a hand and takes off his undershirt." Soon afterward, Peggy grabs her clothes and Trish's, and the two girls run to the bedroom. The boys try to talk them into coming out. Peggy opens the door and bawls them out. The lights fade out on the boys, and this scene begins. You may omit Billy's line when you present this scene.

PEGGY: Show them—What's the matter?

TRISH: I can't do this—

PEGGY: Well, you're doin' it, so shut up.

TRISH: It felt weird playin' so near my parents' bedroom—

PEGGY: They won't come back—

TRISH: I know—

PEGGY: You gotta do it sometime. You're fourteen years old! You wanna wait till you're an old maid—?

TRISH: No—

PEGGY: Don't you like boys?

TRISH: Yeah—

PEGGY: Whaddaya gonna do, wear a "Keep Off—No Trespassing" sign on you your whole life?

TRISH: *No!* I want them to trespass on me! It isn't that—

PEGGY: *What?*

TRISH: Nothin'. There's just somethin' wrong with me, OK? This room's so small.

PEGGY: Don'tya ever think about boys?

TRISH: (*Exasperated*) I think about them all the time!

PEGGY: OK, there's two of 'em out there right now, so what's the— (PEGGY *leaps from one bed to the other, where* TRISH *is sitting.*)

TRISH: (*Exploding*) It's not boys like Boo, or Billy, I think about! I don't lie in bed at night and have dreams about them the way I do about Brian—(*Didn't mean to let it slip out*) —Uh-oh.

PEGGY: Brian?

TRISH: Never mind.

PEGGY: Who's Brian?

TRISH: *Shut up!*

PEGGY: Who's Brian?

TRISH: (*Shamed*) Wilson. In the Beach Boys. I have dreams about him.

PEGGY: Brian? The tall one?

TRISH: They're not regular dreams—

PEGGY: I like the blond one, Dennis? The drummer? He's cute—

TRISH: (*Crazy desperate*) *Shut up!* I'm in love with Brian Wilson! Don't you understand? I love him! I have weird thoughts about him! I could never do anything sexy with a regular boy—

PEGGY: Hey, what's wrong with you? Everybody likes the Beach Boys—

TRISH: It's not like everybody! Leave me alone, I wanna go home—

PEGGY: You *are* home—

TRISH: Oh—

PEGGY: Dufus. What's the big deal? Tons of girls like the Beach Boys—

TRISH: It's not like tons of girls! It's not normal, it's not the way other girls feel, I know it—

PEGGY: It is *so* normal—

TRISH: You call this normal? (*She reaches under her bed and takes out an old photograph album.*)

[BILLY: (*Bellowing*)—Hey, girl—]

Peggy: *Suffer!*—What?

TRISH: It's this picture album we've had in our family a million centuries. My mother passed it down to me the day I entered womanhood. Lookit. That's where I wrote out all the words to "A Thousand Stars in the Sky" by Kathy Young and the Innocents, 'cause it was the first song I ever bought and my mother yelled at me to turn it off after I played it sixty-five times. (*Melodramatic*) That's how I started.

PEGGY: Started what?

TRISH: See those little pictures of my grandma and my grandpa at their wedding? (*Almost in tears*) You can hardly see my grandma's face 'cause I wrote the words to "Surfer Girl" over her. I'm sick. Look. All the words to all the Beach Boys songs, 'cause Brian writes all the songs. Pictures of them, pictures of Brian—(PEGGY *tries to take a closer look, but* TRISH *yanks the album away.*)—And you should see the dreams I have! Talk about *sick*—

PEGGY: You're not sick.

TRISH: I'm not normal.

PEGGY: Don't say that.

TRISH: I'm not normal.

PEGGY: That's not true.

TRISH: I'm not normal.

PEGGY: *Shut up!* You're normal!

TRISH: If I was normal, I wouldn't go around saying I'm not normal; I'm not normal like that. (*She turns and looks out the window.*) Star light, star bright, first star I see tonight . . .

PEGGY: Earth to Trish, earth to Trish. . .

TRISH: (*Whirls around; rapid-fire*) Wish I may, wish I might have the wish I wish tonight.

PEGGY: You're not normal.

Questions for Discussion

1. Why do you think Trish keeps saying she is not normal? Do you think she is? Why? Why does Peggy finally agree that Trish is not normal?

2. Which of the two girls do you empathize with more? Why?

3. Music is important throughout the play. During 1965, the Beach Boys were very popular. Do you think Trish is weird because she fantasizes about being with Brian Wilson? Why or why not?

4. Judging from this short scene, do you think Rimmer presents a glimpse of typical teenagers? Why? Do you think they differ from today's teenagers? Explain.

5. Why is Trish so frightened? Does she have a right to be?

Celia: About 18
Rosalind: About 18
Length of scene: Three minutes and 45 seconds
to four minutes and 15 seconds

As You Like It

William Shakespeare/*England*

Set in France, this play begins with the wicked Duke Frederick usurping his elder brother's throne. The elder duke is now living like Robin Hood in the Forest of Arden. The elder duke is Rosalind's father, so she too is banished from the court. Along with her cousin Celia, Rosalind sets out to find her father.

Another set of brothers also is having a disagreement. Oliver, the elder, is to educate Orlando, but has kept him on a tight rein. Orlando begins to rebel. He matches his strength against the duke's wrestling champion and wins. Instead of being rewarded, he is banished from the court by Frederick.

The two girls, before their own banishment, had attended the wrestling match where Rosalind gave Orlando a chain from around her neck.

The elder duke's court jester, Touchstone, accompanies Rosalind and Celia in their search for the banished duke. For safety's sake, Rosalind has dressed as a boy.

In this scene Rosalind and Celia have just found verses in praise of Rosalind pinned on trees in the forest; they have been reading the verses aloud.

CELIA: Didst thou hear these verses?

ROSALIND: O yes, I heard them all and more too; for some of them had in them more feet than the verses would bear.[1]

CELIA: That's no matter. The feet[2] might bear the verses.

ROSALIND: Ay, but the feet were lame and could not bear[3] themselves without the verse and therefore stood[4] lamely in the verse.

CELIA: But didst thou hear without wondering how thy name should be hanged and carved upon these trees?

ROSALIND: I was seven of the nine days[5] out of the wonder before you came, for look here what I found on a palm tree. I was never so berhymed[6] since Pythagoras'[7] time that I was an Irish rat, which I can hardly remember.

CELIA: Trow[8] you who hath done this?

ROSALIND: Is it a man?

CELIA: And a chain that you once wore, about his neck. Change you color?

ROSALIND: I prithee,[9] who?

CELIA: O Lord, Lord, it is a hard matter for friends to meet. But mountains may be removed with earthquakes and so encounter.

ROSALIND: Nay, but who is it?

CELIA: Is it possible?[10]

---

[1] hold

[2] This is a pun on feet as units of measure; how far the feet of pedestrians would walk.

[3] could not last

[4] stayed

[5] I have endured nearly a nine days' wonder.

[6] so rhymed to death. It was believed that in Ireland rats could be killed with rhymed spells.

[7] A Greek philosopher who believed in the transmigration of soulds after death, that is, that human souls passed into the bodies of animals

[8] know

[9] beg of you

ROSALIND: Nay, I prithee now with most petitionary vehemence,[11] tell me who it is?

CELIA: O wonderful, wonderful and most wonderful wonderful, and yet again wonderful, and after that, out of all whooping![12]

ROSALIND: Good my complexion![13] Dost thou think, though I am caparisoned[14] like a man, I have a doublet and hose in my disposition?[15] One inch of delay more in a South Sea of discovery. I prithee, tell me who is it quickly, and speak apace. I would thou couldst stammer that thou mightst pour this concealed man out of thy mouth as wine comes out of a narrow-mouthed bottle—either too much at once or none at all. I prithee, take the cork out of thy mouth, that I may drink thy tidings.

CELIA: So you may put a man in your belly.

ROSALIND: Is he of God's making?[16] What manner of man? Is his head worth a hat or his chin worth a beard?

CELIA: Nay, he hath but a little beard.

ROSALIND: Why God will send more if the man will be thankful. Let me stay the growth of his beard, if thou delay me not the knowledge of his chin.[17]

CELIA: It is young Orlando that tripped up the wrestler's heels and your heart both in an instant.

ROSALIND: Nay but the devil take mocking! Speak sad brow and true maid.[18]

CELIA: I' faith, coz, 'tis he.

ROSALIND: Orlando?

---

[10] Is it possible not to know?

[11] strongest pleading

[12] beyond any cry of wonder

[13] Temperament or appearance; this is a mild oath.

[14] dressed

[15] nature

[16] Is he a normal person?

[17] I can wait for his beard to grow if you will just tell me whose chin it is.

[18] in earnest truthfulness

CELIA: Orlando.

ROSALIND: Alas the day! What shall I do with my doublet and hose? What did he when thou saw'st him? What said he? How looked he? Wherein went he?[19] What makes he here?[20] Did he ask for me? Where remains he? How parted he with thee? And when shalt thou see him again? Answer me in one word.

CELIA: You must borrow me Gargantua's[21] mouth first, 'tis a word too great for any mouth of this age's size. To say "ay" and "no" to these particulars is more than to answer in a catechism.

ROSALIND: But doth he know that I am in this forest and in man's apparel? Looks he as freshly as he did the day he wrestled?

CELIA: It is as easy to count atomies[22] as to resolve the propositions of a lover,[23] but take a taste of my finding him and relish it[24] with good observance. I found him under a tree like a dropped acorn.

ROSALIND: It may well be called Jove's tree,[25] when it drops such fruit.

CELIA: Give me audience, good madam.

ROSALIND: Proceed.

CELIA: There lay he stretched along like a wounded knight—

ROSALIND: Though it be pity to see such a sight, it well becomes the ground.

CELIA: Cry "holla"[26] the tongue, I prithee; it curvets[27] unseasonably. He was furnished[28] like a hunter—

---

[19] How was he clothed?

[20] What is he doing here?

[21] an enormous giant in the satirical tale of the writer Rabelais, well-known in England at the time

[22] motes in a sunbeam

[23] solve the problems of a lover

[24] whet your appetite for my tale

[25] Jove's tree was the oak, thought to be the "king of trees."

[26] whoa

[27] prances

[28] dressed

ROSALIND: O ominous! He comes to kill my heart.

CELIA: I would sing my song wihout a burden.[29] Thou bring'st me out of tune.

ROSALIND: Do you not know I am a woman? When I think, I must speak. Sweet, say on.

CELIA: You bring me out. Soft.[30] Comes he not here?

ROSALIND: 'Tis he! Slink by and note him.

---

[29] chorus

[30] wait

Questions for Discussion

1. The play is a comedy and, of course, this scene is meant to be humorous. Do you think it is? Why? What contributes to the humor?

2. What do you think is Celia's attitude about the way Rosalind has expressed her feelings of love for Orlando?

3. Rosalind seems to be overwhelmed with eagerness to know who wrote the verses. Since this is the case, why does Celia wait to tell her who it is?

4. What sort of relationship do Rosalind and Celia have? Explain.

5. How would you feel if a boyfriend or girlfriend wrote verses about you and tacked them to a lot of trees? How would your feelings differ from Rosalind's? Why?

Scenes for Two Males

Bob: 18
Timothy: 17
Length of scene: Three minutes to three
minutes and 45 seconds

Scars

Zachary Thomas/*U.S.A.*

T he play takes place both in the 1960s and the early 1980s,
switching back and forth from one time period to another. It
tells the story of two young men who meet in college and,
despite differences, become friends. One of them, Timothy,
wants to be a writer, the other a businessman. Ironically, their
lives become just the reverse.

This scene opens the play, which occurs in a little college
town in Ohio. It is late September.

(*As the lights come up,* TIMOTHY *is kneeling by one of the two single beds, hands clasped, resting on the mattress. He doesn't glance up as* BOB *enters, carrying two suitcases.*)

TIMOTHY: (*Praying*) Our Thomas Wolfe, who art in heaven, hallowed be thy name. Thy novels be read; thy writing be loved in the rest of earth as it is in Carolina.

(*Astounded,* BOB *stops for a moment and then crosses to the other bed. He turns, keeping an eye on* TIMOTHY.)

TIMOTHY: Give us this day our daily prose, and forgive us our writing blocks as we forgive your critics.

(BOB *sets down his suitcases, shaking his head.*)

TIMOTHY: (*Rising and facing* BOB, *he grins.*) There's no god. No heaven, except what we create in our minds. Thomas Wolfe is my god. (*He holds out his hand*) I'm Timothy U. Landis.

BOB: (*Taking his hand*) Hi, Bob Thompson.

TIMOTHY: Since I arrived first, I took this side of the room, this bed, this half of the dresser. (*He points to a large, squat chest of drawers.*)

BOB: Fine, I have no preference.

TIMOTHY: Each one of us has preferences. We simply have to find what they are and not deny them. We have to be true to ourselves.

BOB: (*Placing one of the suitcases atop a student desk by the bed.*) Maybe that's why I'm here. To find out my preferences, what I want out of life. (*He opens the suitcase and pulls out socks and underwear, shoving them into drawers.*)

TIMOTHY: Need any help?

BOB: (*Surprised*) You can hang these up, if you like. (*He hands shirts and jeans to* TIMOTHY.)

TIMOTHY: (*Taking the clothes to the closet*) I'm aware of my preferences. All of them. I know what I want. (*He drapes a shirt around a hanger, shaping it just right so there are no wrinkles.*)

BOB: That's wonderful. But if that's the case, why are you even here?

TIMOTHY: Scoff, if you want to. (*He hangs up the pants.*) But I'm going to be a writer (*He sighs deeply.*) I may not last here, I don't know. I'll see what they have to show me. If it's nothing I like, I'll go south to the country where Wolfe was reared.

BOB: (*Sounding puzzled*) Thomas Wolfe? I've heard the name—

TIMOTHY: (*Self mocking*) That's right. My lord and god.

BOB: You're serious about that, aren't you?

TIMOTHY: (*He takes a few other shirts from* BOB *and returns to the closet.*) Of course.

(BOB *shuts the first suitcase, slides it under the bed and opens the other.*)

TIMOTHY: (*Hanging up the shirts*) I've been told that for freshman English, each person is required to do a final project. It can be a piece of fiction. I've written mine, a novella, I admit, influenced by my god. I showed it to the head of the department. He said it was more like a creative thesis for an MFA.

(*The lights dim as* BOB *crosses downstage.*)

BOB: (*Addressing the audience*) I wondered what I'd gotten into, realizing the first of many contradictions. I found Timothy likeable, yet bizarre.

(*The lights dim and in a moment come up in the bedroom.* BOB *is lying in bed, wide awake as* TIMOTHY *enters*)

BOB: Tim?

TIMOTHY: Timothy U. (*Laughs*) What are you doing awake, Robert? Don't you have an eight o'clock class?

BOB: It's Bob! (*Shrugging*) Oh, all right . . . Robert.

TIMOTHY: (*Surprised*) Robert?

BOB: (*Smiles*) I'm losing the war. School's been in session—what is it— a month? I haven't convinced you. I never will; I give up. My name is Robert and yours is Timothy U.

TIMOTHY: Sorry.

BOB: To answer your question, Yes, I do have an eight o'clock. A damned econ class.

TIMOTHY: Did I wake you?

BOB: (*Throwing back the covers, he swings his feet to the floor and reaches for a glass of water on the seat of the desk chair.*) No you didn't wake me. At least the noise didn't wake me. It's the anticipation, I guess. Because I know that—

TIMOTHY: Sooner or later, usually later . . . (*He laughs.*) Sooner or later, I'll be back.

BOB: It's none of my business.

TIMOTHY: Of course, it's your business. We're roommates . . . friends too?

BOB: Sure, friends.

TIMOTHY: And if I'm keeping you awake—

BOB: Damn it, Timothy.

TIMOTHY: Timothy U.

BOB: (*Laughing almost hysterically*) All right, for God's sake, Timothy U.

TIMOTHY: You're tired. Too tired. After this I'll try to make less noise.

BOB: Hell, you don't make any noise now. It's just that—

TIMOTHY: What?

BOB: Where do you go every night? They roll up the sidewalks at ten. The town is dry, for God's sake. There aren't even bars. If there were—

TIMOTHY: I'm not old enough? (*He stands and crosses to his side of the room.*) You're right. Anyhow, I have no interest in bars. (*Sitting on his own bed, facing* BOB) I go to a cemetery.

BOB: What!

TIMOTHY: That's right. Just outside town. It's quiet and peaceful. There are these graves. Young men, sixteen, eighteen, twenty, twenty-one. It gives me inspiration. I wouldn't tell that to anyone else, but I know I can trust you.

BOB: (*Chuckling*) Yes, you can trust me.

TIMOTHY: I've been writing this poem. An epic. The life of Thomas Wolfe.

BOB: (*Smiling, not unkindly*) Timothy U., you're crazy.

Questions for Discussion

1. Do you think Timothy really believes what he says about the writer Thomas Wolfe? Why? Why do you suppose he would go to a cemetery to be among the graves of young men?

2. Why do you think Timothy said he knew all his preferences? What do you think he meant by that?

3. What sorts of feelings do you suppose Bob has about his roommate? How would you feel if you had to live with someone like Timothy?

4. What qualities does Bob have that allow him to be so understanding about Timothy's idiosyncrasies?

5. Would you guess that Timothy is a talented writer or not? Explain.

Valentine: 18 to 20
Proteus: 18 to 20
Length of scene: Three minutes to three
minutes and 30 seconds

Two Gentlemen of Verona

William Shakespeare/*England*

This is one of the least complex of Shakespeare's comedies. The plot revolves around the fact that Valentine has fallen in love with Silvia, only to have his best friend Proteus, who supposedly loved Julia, attempt to thwart the romance.

This is the scene that opens the play. Valentine sets out to seek honor at the Emperor's court in Milan, while Proteus stays home to seek success in his love of Julia, who has many suitors.

(*Enter* VALENTINE *and* PROTEUS.)

VALENTINE: Cease to persuade, my loving Proteus.
　　Home-keeping youth[1] have ever homely wits.
　　Were 't not affection chains thy tender days
　　To the sweet glances of thy honored love,
　　I rather would entreat thy company
　　To see the wonders of the world abroad,
　　Than, living dully sluggardized[2] at home,
　　Wear out thy youth with shapeless[3] idleness.
　　But since thou lovest, love still, and thrive therein.
　　Even as I would when I to love begin.

PROTEUS: Wilt thou be gone? Sweet Valentine, adieu!
　　Think on thy Proteus when thou haply[4] seest
　　Some rare noteworthy object in thy travel.
　　Wish me partaker in thy happiness
　　When thou dost meet good hap,[5] and in thy danger—
　　If ever danger do environ[6] thee—
　　Commend thy grievance to my holy prayers,
　　For I will be thy beadsman,[7] Valentine.

VALENTINE: And on a love-book[8] pray for my success?

PROTEUS: Upon some book I love I'll pray for thee.

VALENTINE: That's on some shallow story of deep love,
　　How young Leander crossed the Hellespont.[9]

PROTEUS: That's a deep story of a deeper love,
　　For he was more than over shoes in love.

VALENTINE: 'Tis true, for you are over boots in love,
　　And yet you never swum the Hellespont.

PROTEUS: Over the boots? Nay, give me not the
　　boots.[10]

---

[1] A youth who is a "stay-at-home."
[2] living like a dull sluggard
[3] without purpose
[4] by chance
[5] luck
[6] surround
[7] a person who prays for a benefactor
[8] a book about love
[9] In Greek legend, the young lover who drowned swimming the Hellespont to reach Hero.
[10] don't make fun of me

VALENTINE: No. I will not, for it boots[11] thee not.

PROTEUS: What?

VALENTINE: To be in love, where scorn is bought with
    groans.
    Coy looks with heart-sore sighs, one fading moment's
    mirth
    With twenty watchful, weary, tedious nights.
    If haply won, perhaps a hapless[12] gain;
    If lost, why then a grievous labor won;
    However, but a folly bought with wit,
    Or else a wit by folly vanquishèd.

PROTEUS: So, by your circumstance,[13] you call me fool.

VALENTINE: So, by your circumstance, I fear you'll prove.

PROTEUS: 'Tis love you cavil at.[14] I am not Love.

VALENTINE: Love is your master, for he masters you;
    And he that is so yokèd by a fool,
    Methinks, should not be chronicled[15] for wise.

PROTEUS: Yet writers say, as in the sweetest bud
    The eating canker[16] dwells, so eating love
    Inhabits in the finest wits of all.

VALENTINE: And writers say, as the most forward[17] bud
    Is eaten by the canker ere it blow,[18]
    Even so by love the young and tender wit
    Is turned to folly, blasting[19] in the bud,
    Losing his verdure even in the prime,[20]
    And all the fair effects of future hopes.
    But wherefore waste I time to counsel thee,
    That art a votary[21] to fond desire?
    Once more adieu! My father at the road[22]

---

[11] profits
[12] unlucky
[13] roundabout argument
[14] object to
[15] recorded
[16] worm
[17] the earliest
[18] before the bud fully blossoms
[19] withering
[20] springtime
[21] devoted to
[22] harbor

Expects my coming, there to see me shipped.

PROTEUS: And thither will I bring thee, Valentine.

VALENTINE: Sweet Proteus, no. Now let us take our
      leave.
   To Milan let me hear from thee by letters
   Of thy success in love, and what news else
   Betideth[23] here in absence of thy friend,
   And I likewise will visit thee with mine.

PROTEUS: All happiness bechance[24] to thee in Milan!

VALENTINE: As much to you at home! And so, farewell.

   (*Exit.*)

PROTEUS. He after honor hunts, I after love.
   He leaves his friends to dignify[25] them more:
   I leave myself, my friends, and all, for love.
   Thou, Julia, thou hast metamorphosed me,[26]
   Made me neglect my studies, lose my time,
   War with good counsel,[27] set the world at naught,
   Made wit with musing weak, heart sick with
      thought.

Questions for Discussion

1.   What sort of relationship do Valentine and Proteus appear to have?
     Explain by pointing to specific lines that show this.

2.   What sort of honor do you think Valentine could be seeking by
     going to Milan?

3.   Suppose the dialogue was changed to contemporary English. Do
     you think it would be realistic for friends to say the things to each
     other that Valentine and Proteus say? Explain.

4.   By what happens in this scene, do you think you would like to
     know the outcome of the play? Why?

5.   Do you identify with either Proteus or Valentine? Why?

---

[23] occurs
[24] befall
[25] bring honor to
[26] changed me into another shape
[27] advice

David: 18
Marvin: 18
Length of scene: Four minutes 45 seconds to
five minutes 45 seconds

Enter Laughing

Joseph Stein/ *U.S.A.*

(*Adapted from the novel by Carl Reiner*)

The play is based on Carl Reiner's autobiographical novel about growing up in the Bronx in the 1930s. The central character is David, who works as a delivery boy in a sewing factory and whose family wants him to be a pharmacist.

David has other ideas. He auditions for a semi-professional theatre company, which, as it turns out, casts anyone who will pay partial "tuition" to learn acting. The rest of the money such training would cost, or so says the man who heads the company, is paid by a scholarship.

Along the way to being a terrible actor in the first production, David is juggling girlfriends. There's Miss B., who already is betrothed, the daughter of the theatre company's manager, and Wanda.

This scene occurs near the beginning of the play, just after Mr. Foreman, David's boss, has told him a girl called, but he can't remember the name. The title of the play comes from the fact that when asked to read the dialogue of a certain character, he reads the stage direction, as well. Of course, it is "Enter laughing."

(MARVIN *enters.* MARVIN *is* DAVID'S *age; he is not too good-looking, a little timid, unsure of himself. He admires* DAVID, *just this side of hero worship. He carries his lunch, wrapped in a newspaper.*)

DAVID: Hi, Marv.

MARVIN: Hi. (*Crossing to left of table, gets chair from upper left, moves it to left of table. Sits and eats.*)

DAVID: I'm calling Wanda. (*Into phone*) Hello, Wanda? Did you call me? . . . He told me . . . No, he went out . . . Yeah, Marvin just came down. He's having his lunch . . . Saturday night? Gee, I'd love to, Wanda, only my mother and father are visiting some relatives in Flatbush, and I've got to mind my stupid kid sister. Who's giving the dance? . . . Well, listen, Wanda, maybe after the dance, you and me could get together and have a little tete-a-tete. (*Imitating Ronald Colman.*) "It will be a far, far better thing that you and I will do on Saturday night than has ever been done before.". . . Yes, Ronald Colman, that's right! . . . Goodbye. (*Hangs up and moves chair from upper right to stage right of table.*)

MARVIN: Boy, the way you do those imitations. You're great, you know that, Dave? (DAVID *then goes into a Louis Armstrong routine in midst of which* MARVIN *says: "Louis Armstrong." At end of it he takes rag from bench and dabs face.*) Great!

DAVID: I know. (*He sits right of table.*)

MARVIN: And the way you talk to girls. Boy, I wish I had a steady girl, like you.

DAVID: You do?

MARVIN: I sure do. A steady girl, boy.

DAVID: I'll tell you, Marv, even though I got a steady girl, I think about other girls.

MARVIN: You do?

DAVID: Yeah, a lot. Do you think about girls a lot?

MARVIN: Me? I don't know what you mean by a lot. Sometimes I think about other things.

DAVID: Like what?

MARVIN: (*Considers.*) Oh, you know, other things—food.

DAVID: (*Rises. Crosses left below table, above it, then to stage right of it.*) I think about girls a lot. I admit it. Like if I'm walking down the street, I see a girl swinging along—you know the way they do when they're walking, the way they walk.

MARVIN: Yeah—

DAVID: (*Crossing upstage and downstage*) Sometimes I go two, three blocks out of way, just to watch the way they walk. What the heck, it's better than looking at nothing. Right?

MARVIN: Me, too.

DAVID: (*Upstage center of table.*) I think about it a lot. Like there's this bookkeeper at the LaTesh Hat Company. Her name is Miss B., she's the most zaftig thing you ever saw, Marv, I mean it—

MARVIN: Her name is Miss B.?

DAVID: (*At right of stage right chair.*) That's what they call her. Anyway, she'd drive you crazy if her name was Irving. I go up there sometimes I forget to get a receipt.

MARVIN: I thought you're crazy about Wanda.

DAVID: I am. I'm crazy about Wanda. And I'm crazy about Miss B. And I'm crazy about strange girls on the street. Sometimes I think I'm a sex maniac.

MARVIN: Yeah, me, too.

DAVID: (*Crossing right to upper right. Then downstage*) Only one thing, I talk a lot, but I don't do anything. Not that I don't want to, I just don't. (*Sits chair right of table.*) I'm a big talker.

MARVIN: Me, too.

DAVID: (*Rises above table.*) Another thing. What am I doing in this crummy job? I mean, okay, just for a while, but Mr. Foreman thinks I want to learn the business—what do I want to be a machinist on ladies hats for? (*Picks up two files from table.*)

MARVIN: Then don't.

DAVID: Okay, then why don't I tell him? He keeps saying, you'll work hard, be a good machinist, and I say, sure, Mr. Foreman. . . .

MARVIN: Do you want an apple?

DAVID: No. (*Drumming on shelves with files.*) And my parents, they want me to be a druggist. (*Drums.*) They want me to register in night school for September, to be a druggist. (*Drums.*) I don't want to be a druggist.

MARVIN: Then why don't you tell them?

DAVID: (*Drumming.*) I did tell them. I kind of told them. So they say, what do you want to be? You can't be a nothing. Everyone calls me a nothing. (*Throws files in tray on table. Sits stage right of table.*)

MARVIN: Why don't you want to be a druggist?

DAVID: Because I don't want to. Does everybody have to want to be a druggist?

MARVIN: You know, I wouldn't mind being a druggist.

DAVID: You? You'd poison the whole neighborhood. (*Rises to upstage center of table.*) The thing is, I want to be something. Something, so people will say, there goes Dave Kolovitz, the something.

MARVIN: What's the matter with "there goes the druggist"?

DAVID: (*Crosses right*) Naah.

MARVIN: (*Offering apple.*) You sure you don't want an apple?

DAVID: (*Crosses to above table.*) What's with you and the apple? What's it got, worms or something?

MARVIN: No, my mother just put in two today, that's all. (*Bites second apple.*)

DAVID: (*Crosses left above table to left of table.*) If I had any guts, I'd pack up and go to Panama or someplace.

MARVIN: Why don't you?

DAVID: (*At stage left shouts.*) Because I have to mind my stupid kid sister Saturday night, that's why.

MARVIN: (*Rises, steps left to* DAVID *with apple.*) Okay, you don't have to bite my head off.

DAVID: (*Pause.*) Give me the apple.

MARVIN: I bit it already.

DAVID: What are you giving me an apple for and then eating it yourself?

MARVIN: It ain't my fault you don't know what you want to be.

DAVID: Did I say I don't know what I want to be? I know what I want to be.

MARVIN: Yeah—a something!

DAVID: (*Crosses right below table to right of table.*) No. I'll tell you what I want to be. I want to be an actor.

MARVIN: An actor?

DAVID: (*Crosses downstage right of table.*) Sure. Why not? An actor! (*Faces audience, poses.*)

MARVIN: You know something? You'd be great!

DAVID: I know. But you can't just be an actor. You can't just go around and tell people—hello, I'm an actor!

MARVIN: (*crossing right to* DAVID.) Hey, I saw this ad in today's paper. I saw it yesterday, too. I saw it both days.

DAVID: An ad? For what?

MARVIN: For actors.

DAVID: For actors?

MARVIN: For actors.

DAVID: You're crazy! (*Goes upstage, takes newspaper from shelf on center wall.* MARVIN *crosses left of table to above it.*)

MARVIN: (*Taking paper from* DAVID, *finds ad.*) It's here, right here in the paper. I saw it yesterday, I saw it today. . . . Here. When I saw it I even thought about you.

DAVID: (*Reads; upstage of stage right chair.*) "Marlowe Theatre and School for Dramatic Arts . . . Scholarships for Promising Young Actors . . . "

MARVIN: (*At stage left of* DAVID.) Just do your Ronald Colman or your Humphrey Bogart.

DAVID: "Learn to act before audiences."

MARVIN: No kidding, you're a cinch.

DAVID: (*Crossing stage right.* MARVIN *follows.*) They'll see applicants at six o'clock.

MARVIN: What do you say, will you go?

DAVID: Sure. Why not?

MARVIN: Bet you a dime you don't.

DAVID: It's a bet.

(*They shake hands.*)

MARVIN: (*Gets apple from table.*) Here, I only took one bite.

DAVID: Thanks—I can't make it, though. I don't get out of here till six o'clock—

MARVIN: Listen, you don't want to be a machinist or a druggist all your life?

DAVID: Besides, I got to get home tonight. What will I tell my mother?

MARVIN: Okay, okay, you lose; give me the dime.

DAVID: Besides it's in the paper. There'll be a thousand guys.

MARVIN: Okay, give me the dime.

Questions for Discussion

1. The play, of course, is a comedy. What contributes to the humor in this scene?

2. Even though David has a steady girlfriend, he is interested in other girls too. Why do you think this is so?

3. What type of person is Marvin? Do you like him? Do you identify with him? Why?

4. Why do you suppose Marvin keeps offering David the apple?

5. What do you suppose David does not want to be a pharmacist? Do you agree with his reasons? Why?

Carr: 17
Mio: 17
Length of scene: Five minutes and 15 seconds
to six minutes and 15 seconds

Winterset

Maxwell Anderson/ *U.S.A.*

The play, written largely in poetic form, represents the tragedy of modern life, and is based in part on a real trial of the 1920s. But the play, written in 1935, goes far beyond the factual courtroom to expound its theme of social injustice, renunciation, and revenge.

Mio Romagna, son of a radical who was executed for a crime he did not commit, is consumed with wanting to clear his father's name. He's seeking Garth, the only witness who could help.

The play also is a tragic love story involving Mio and Miriamne, Garth's sister.

In this scene, Mio meets up with a friend, Carr. You can skip the dialogue involving Miriamne, if you wish, and simply pretend another character is there and then leaves.

CARR: Thought you said you were never coming east again.

MIO: Yeah, but—I heard something changed my mind.

CARR: Same old business?

MIO: Yes. Just as soon not talk about it.

CARR: Where did you go from Portland?

MIO: Fishing—I went fishing. God's truth.

CARR: Right after I left?

MIO: Fell in with a fisherman's family on the coast and went after the beautiful mackerel fish that swim in the beautiful sea. Family of Greeks—Aristides Marinos was his lovely name. He sang while he fished. Made the pea-green Pacific ring with his Greek chanties. Then I went to Hollywood High School for a while.

CARR: I'll bet that's a seat of learning.

MIO: It's the hind end of all wisdom. They kicked me out after a time.

CARR: For cause?

MIO: Because I had no permanent address, you see. That means nobody's paying school taxes for you, so out you go. (*To* MIRIAMNE) What's the matter, kid?

[MIRIAMNE: Nothing. (*She looks up at him and they pause for a moment.*) Nothing.]

MIO: I'm sorry.

[MIRIAMNE: It's all right. (*She withdraws her eyes from his and goes out past him. He turns and looks after her.*)]

CARR: Control your chivalry.

MIO: A pretty kid.

CARR: A baby.

MIO: Wait for me.

CARR: Be a long wait? (MIO *steps swiftly out after* MIRIAMNE, *then returns.*) Yeah?

MIO: She's gone.

CARR: Think of that.

MIO: No, but I mean—vanished. Presto—into nothing— prodigioso.

CARR: Damn good thing, if you ask me. The homely ones are bad enough, but the lookers are fatal.

MIO: You exaggerate, Carr.

CARR: I doubt it.

MIO: Well, let her go. This riverbank's loaded with typhus rats, too. Might as well die one death as another.

CARR: They say chronic alcoholism is nice but expensive. You can always starve to death.

MIO: Not always. I tried it. After the second day I walked thirty miles to Niagara Falls and made a tour of the plant to get the sample of shredded wheat biscuit on the way out.

CARR: Last time I saw you you couldn't think of anything you wanted to do except curse God and pass out. Still feeling low?

MIO: Not much different. (*He turns away, then comes back.*) Talk about the lost generation, I'm the only one fits that title. When the State executes your father, and your mother dies of grief, and you know damn well he was innocent, and the authorities of your hometown politely inform you they'd consider it a favor if you lived somewhere else—that cuts you off from the world—with a meat-axe.

CARR: They asked you to move?

MIO: It came to that.

CARR: God, that was white of them.

MIO: It probably gave them a headache just to see me after all that agitation. They knew as well as I did my father never staged a holdup. Anyway, I've got a new interest in life now.

CARR: Yes—I saw her.

MIO: I don't mean the skirt—No, I got wind of something, out west, some college professor investigating the trial and turning up new evidence. Couldn't find anything he'd written out there, so I beat it east and arrived on this blessed island just in time to find the bums holing up in the public library for the winter. I know now what the unemployed have been doing since the depression started. They've been catching up on their reading in the main reference room. Man, what a stench! Maybe I stank, too, but a hobo has the stench of ten because his shoes are poor.

CARR: Tennyson.

MIO: Right. Jeez, I'm glad we met again! Never knew anybody else that could track me through the driven snow of Victorian literature.

CARR: Now you're cribbing from some half-forgotten criticism of Ben Jonson's Roman plagiarisms.

MIO: Where did you get your education, sap?

CARR: Not in the public library, sap. My father kept a newsstand.

MIO: Well, you're right again. (*There is a faint rumble of thunder.*) What's that? Winter thunder?

CARR: Or Mister God, beating on His little tocsin. Maybe announcing the advent of a new social order.

MIO: Or maybe it's going to rain coffee and doughnuts.

CARR: Or maybe it's going to rain.

MIO: Seems more likely. (*Lowering his voice*) Anyhow, I found Professor Hobhouse's discussion of the Romagna case. I think he has something. It occurred to me I might follow it up by doing a little sleuthing on my own account.

CARR: Yes?

MIO: I have done a little. And it leads me to somewhere in the tenement house that backs up against the bridge. That's how I happen to be here.

CARR: They'll never let you get anywhere with it, Mio. I told you that before.

MIO: I know you did.

CARR: The State can't afford to admit it was wrong, you see. Not when there's been that much of a row kicked up over it. So for all practical purposes the State was right and your father robbed the payroll.

MIO: There's still such a thing as evidence.

CARR: It's something you can buy. In fact, at the moment I don't think of anything you can't buy, including life, honor, virtue, glory, public office, conjugal affection and all kinds of justice, from the traffic court to the immortal nine. Go out and make yourself a pot of money and you can buy all the justice you want. Convictions obtained, convictions averted. Lowest rates in years.

MIO: I know all that.

CARR: Sure.

MIO: This thing didn't happen to you.
They've left you your name
and whatever place you can take. For my heritage
they've left me with one thing only, and that's to be
my father's voice crying up out of the earth
and quicklime where they stuck him. Electrocution
doesn't kill, you know. They eviscerate them
with a turn of the knife in the dissecting room.
The blood spurts out. The man was alive. Then into
the lime pit, leave no trace. Make it short shrift
and chemical dissolution. That's what they thought
of the man that was my father. Then my mother—
I tell you these county burials are swift and cheap
and run for profit! Out of the house
and into the ground, you wife of a dead dog. Wait,
here's some Romagna spawn left. Something crawls here—
something they called a son. Why couldn't he die
along with his mother? Well, ease him out of town,
ease him out, boys, and see you're not too gentle.
He might come back. And, by their own living Jesus,
I will go back and hang the carrion
around their necks that made it!
Maybe I can sleep then.
Or even live.

CARR: You have to try it?

MIO: Yes.
Yes. It won't let me alone. I've tried to live
and forget—but I was birthmarked with hot iron
into the entrails. I've got to find out who did it
and make them see it till it scalds their eyes
and make them admit it till their tongues are blistered
with saying how black they lied!

Questions for Discussion

1. Why do you think the playwright used such high-blown language
   for this play? Do you think it is effective? Why?

2. Is Mio a believable 17-year-old? Why?

3. Do you think it logical that Mio is so consumed with finding the
   person responsible for his father's execution? Explain.

Eugene: Almost 15
Stan: 18½
Length of scene: Four minutes and 30 seconds
to five minutes and 30 seconds

Brighton Beach Memoirs

Neil Simon/*U.S.A.*

Simon is probably the most popular playwright of this century. His comedies have been running on Broadway regularly since 1960, with several adapted for film and television, for example, *The Odd Couple, Barefoot in the Park,* and *The Sunshine Boys.*

This play takes place in 1937 in Brighton Beach, Brooklyn. The family is having a rough time financially with Eugene's father forced to work two jobs. As the scene shows, his brother Stan will be fired unless he writes a letter of apology.

This scene comes fairly early in the play. Up until this point, Eugene, the central character and narrator, has shown his obsession both with the New York Yankees baseball team and with his cousin Laurie.

STAN (*In half whisper*): Hey! Eugie!

EUGENE: Hi, Stan! (*To the audience*) My brother Stan. He's okay. You'll like him. (*To* STAN) What are you doing home so early?

STAN (*Looks around, lowers his voice*): Is Pop home yet?

EUGENE: No . . . Did you ask about the tickets?

STAN: What tickets?

EUGENE: For the Yankee game. You said your boss knew this guy who could get passes. You didn't ask him?

STAN: Me and my boss had other things to talk about. (*He sits on the steps, his head down, almost in tears*) I'm in trouble, Eug. I mean, really big trouble.

EUGENE (*To the audience*): This really shocked me. Because Stan is the kind of guy who could talk himself out of *any* kind of trouble. (*To* STAN) What kind of trouble?

STAN: I got fired today!

EUGENE (*Shocked*): Fired? You mean for good?

STAN: You don't get fired temporarily. It's permanent. It's a lifetime firing.

EUGENE: Why? What happened?

STAN: It was on account of Andrew. The colored guy who sweeps up. Well, he was cleaning the floor in the stockroom and he lays his broom against the table to put some junk in the trash can and the broom slips, knocks a can of linseed oil over the table and ruins three brand-new hats right out of the box. Nine-dollar Stetsons. It wasn't his fault. He didn't put the linseed oil there, right?

EUGENE: Right.

STAN: So Mr. Stroheim sees the oily hats and he gets crazy. He says to Andrew the hats are going to have to come out of his salary. Twenty-seven dollars. So Andrew starts to cry.

EUGENE: He cried?

STAN: Forty-two years old, he's bawling all over the stockroom. I mean, the man hasn't got too much furniture upstairs anyway, but he's real sweet. He brings me coffee, always laughing, telling me jokes. I never understand them but I laugh anyway, make him feel good, you know?

EUGENE: Yeah?

STAN: Anyway, I said to Mr. Stroheim I didn't think that was fair. It wasn't Andrew's fault.

EUGENE (*Astounded*): You said that to him?

STAN: Sure, why not? So Mr. Stroheim says, "You wanna pay for the hats, big mouth?" So I said, "No. I don't want to pay for the hats." So he says, "Then mind your own business, big mouth."

EUGENE: Holy mackerel.

STAN: So Mr. Stroheim looks at me like machine-gun bullets are coming out of his eyes. And then he calmly sends Andrew over to the factory to pick up three new hats. Which is usually my job. So guess what Mr. Stroheim tells *me* to do?

EUGENE: What?

STAN: He tells me to sweep up. He says, for this week I'm the cleaning man.

EUGENE: I can't believe it.

STAN: Everybody is watching me now, waiting to see what I'm going to do. (EUGENE *nods in agreement*) Even Andrew stopped crying and watched. I felt the dignity of everyone who worked in that store was in my hands. So I grit my teeth and I pick up the broom, and there's this big pile of dirt right in the middle of the floor . . .

EUGENE: Yeah?

STAN: . . . and I sweep it all over Mr. Stroheim's shoes. Andrew had just finished shining them this morning, if you want to talk about irony.

EUGENE: I'm dying. I'm actually dying.

STAN (*Enjoying himself*): You could see everyone in the place is about to bust a gut. Mrs. Mulcahy, the bookkeeper, can hardly keep her false teeth in her mouth. Andrew's eyes are hanging five inches out of their sockets.

EUGENE: This is the greatest story in the history of the world.

STAN: So Mr. Stroheim grabs me and pulls me into his back office, closes the door and pulls down the shades. He gives me this whole story how he was brought up in Germany to respect his superiors. That if he ever—(*With an accent*) "did soch a ting like you do, dey would beat me in der kopf until dey carried me away dead."

EUGENE: That's perfect You got him down perfect.

STAN: And I say, "Yeah. But we're not in Germany, old buddy."

EUGENE: You said that to him?

STAN: No. To myself. I didn't want to go too far.

EUGENE: I was wondering.

STAN: Anyway, he says he's always liked me and always thought I was a good boy and that he was going to give me one more chance. He wants a letter of apology. And that if the letter of apology isn't on his desk by nine o'clock tomorrow morning, I can consider myself fired.

EUGENE: I would have had a heart attack . . . What did you say?

STAN: I said I was not going to apologize if Andrew still had to pay for the hats . . . He said that was between him and Andrew, and that he expected the letter from me in the morning . . . I said good night, walked out of his office, got my hat and went home . . . ten minutes early.

EUGENE: I'm sweating. I swear to God, I'm sweating all over.

STAN: I don't know why I did it. But I got so mad. It just wasn't fair. I mean, if you give in when you're eighteen and a half, you'll give in for the rest of your life, don't you think?

EUGENE: I suppose so . . . So what's the decision? Are you going to write the letter?

STAN: (*Thinks*): . . . No!

EUGENE: Positively?

STAN: Positively. Except I'll have to discuss it with Pop. I know we need the money. But he told me once, you always have to do what you think is right in this world and stand up for your principles.

EUGENE: And what if he says he thinks you're wrong? That you should write the letter.

STAN: He won't. He's gonna leave it up to me, I know it.

EUGENE: But what if he says, "Write the letter"?

STAN: Well, that's something we won't know until after dinner, will we?

(*He walks into the house*)

EUGENE (*Looks after him, then turns to the audience*): All in all, it was shaping up to be one heck of a dinner. I'll say this though—I always had this two-way thing about my brother. Either I worshiped the ground he walked on or I hated him so much I wanted to kill him . . . I guess you know how I feel about him today.

Questions for Discussion

1. Why does Eugene think that what Stan says "is the greatest story in the history of the world"?

2. Considering the circumstances, what do you think Stan should do about the letter? What would you do if you were in his place?

3. Do you like Eugene and Stan? Can you identify with them? Why?

4. Why do you suppose Simon has Eugene serve both as a character in the play and as a narrator who talks directly to the audience? Do you think this is effective?

5. What does Eugene mean by the final line about his brother? Do you think most younger brothers have ambivalent feelings about siblings?

Lone: 20
Ma: 18
Length of scene: Five minutes and 15 seconds
to six minutes and 15 seconds

The Dance and the Railroad

David Henry Hwang/ *U.S.A.*

The play takes place in 1867 when Chinese men worked as laborers on the transcontinental railroad. Hwang makes a powerful statement about their exploitation in having to perform back-breaking jobs for many hours each day with little pay. The action takes place during a strike against the railroad.

The Dance and the Railroad tells of Lone, who studied eight years to be an opera performer and who then had to drop out of school to make money for his family. In addition to being a statement about exploitation, the drama is also a statement about artists having to do other work in order to survive. Lone will not give up his dream, and goes to the mountain every night to practice. In the opening scene, Ma sneaks up to watch Lone and asks him to perform for the men at camp. Lone tells Ma that he's a bothersome insect who should just "fly away."

This excerpt is from Scene II.

MA: Hey.

LONE: You? Again?

MA: I forgive you.

LONE: You . . . what?

MA: For making fun of me yesterday. I forgive you.

LONE: You can't—

MA: No. Don't thank me.

LONE: You can't forgive me.

MA: No. Don't mention it.

LONE: You—! I never asked for your forgiveness.

MA: I know. That's just the kinda guy I am.

LONE: This is ridiculous. Why don't you leave? Go down to your friends and play soldiers, sing songs, tell stories.

MA: Ah! See? That's just it. I got other ways I wanna spend my time. Will you teach me the opera?

LONE: What?

MA: I wanna learn it. I dreamt about it all last night.

LONE: No.

MA: The dance, the opera—I can do it.

LONE: You think so?

MA: Yeah. When I get outa here, I wanna go back to China and perform.

LONE: You want to become an actor?

MA: Well, I wanna perform.

LONE: Don't you remember the story about the three sons whose parents send them away to learn a trade? After three years, they return. The first one says, "I have become a coppersmith." The parents say, "Good. Second son, what have you become?" "I've become a silversmith." "Good—and youngest son, what about you?" "I have become an actor." When the parents hear that their son has become only an actor, they are very sad. The mother beats her head against the ground until the ground, out of pity, opens up and swallows her. The father is so angry he can't even speak, and the anger builds up inside him until it blows his body to pieces—little bits of his skin are found hanging from trees days later. You don't know how you endanger your relatives by becoming an actor.

MA: Well, I don't wanna become an "actor." That sounds terrible. I just wanna perform. Look, I'll be rich by the time I get out of here, right?

LONE: Oh?

MA: Sure. By the time I go back to China, I'll ride in gold sedan chairs, with twenty wives fanning me all around.

LONE: Twenty wives? This boy is ambitious.

MA: I'll give out pigs on New Year's and keep a stable of small birds to give to any woman who pleases me. And in my spare time, I'll perform.

LONE: Between your twenty wives and your birds, where will you find a free moment?

MA: I'll play Gwan Gung and tell stories of what life was like on the Gold Mountain.

LONE: Ma, just how long have you been in "America"?

MA: Huh? About four weeks.

LONE: You are a big dreamer.

MA: Well, all us ChinaMen here are—right? Men with little dreams—have little brains to match. They walk with their eyes down, trying to find extra grains of rice on the ground.

LONE: So, you know all about "America"? Tell me, what kind of stories will you tell?

MA: I'll say, "We laid tracks like soldiers. Mountains? We hung from cliffs in baskets and the winds blew us like birds. Snow? We lived underground like moles for days at a time. Deserts? We—"

LONE: Wait. Wait. How do you know these things after only four weeks?

MA: They told me—the other ChinaMen on the gang. We've been telling stories ever since the strike began.

LONE: They make it sound like it's very enjoyable.

MA: They said it is.

LONE: Oh? And you believe them?

MA: They're my friends. Living underground in winter—sounds exciting, huh?

LONE: Did they say anything about the cold?

MA: Oh, I already know about that. They told me about the mild winters and the warm snow.

LONE: Warm snow?

MA: When I go home, I'll bring some back to show my brothers.

LONE: Bring some—? On the boat?

MA: They'll be shocked—they never seen American snow before.

LONE: You can't. By the time you get snow to the boat, it'll have melted, evaporated, and returned as rain already.

MA: No.

LONE: No?

MA: Stupid.

LONE: Me?

MA: You been here awhile, haven't you?

LONE: Yes. Two years.

MA: Then how come you're so stupid? This is the Gold Mountain. The snow here doesn't melt. It's not wet.

LONE: That's what they told you?

MA: Yeah. It's true.

LONE: Did anyone show you any of this snow?

MA: No. It's not winter.

LONE: So where does it go?

MA: Huh?

LONE: Where does it go, if it doesn't melt? What happens to it?

MA: The snow? I dunno. I guess it just stays around.

LONE: So where is it? Do you see any?

MA: Here? Well, no, but . . . (*Pause*) This is probably one of those places where it doesn't snow—even in winter.

LONE: Oh.

MA: Anyway, what's the use of me telling you what you already know?

Hey, c'mon—teach me some of that stuff. Look—I've been practicing the walk—how's this? (*Demonstrates*)

LONE: You look like a duck in heat.

MA: Hey—it's a start, isn't it?

LONE: Tell you what—you want to play some *die siu*?

MA: *Die siu*? Sure.

LONE: You know, I'm pretty good.

MA: Hey, I play with the guys at camp. You can't be any better than Lee—he's really got it down. (LONE *pulls out a case with two dice.*)

LONE: I used to play till morning.

MA: Hey, us too. We see the sun start to rise, and say, "Hey, if we go to sleep now, we'll never get up for work." So we just keep playing.

LONE: (*Holding out dice*) *Die* or *siu*?

MA: *Siu*.

LONE: You sure?

MA: Yeah!

LONE: All right. (*He rolls.*) *Die!*

MA: *Siu!*

(*They see the result.*)

MA: Not bad.

(*They continue taking turns rolling through the following section;* MA *always loses.*)

LONE: I haven't touched these in two years.

MA: I gotta practice more.

LONE: Have you lost much money?

MA: Huh? So what?

LONE: Oh, you have gold hidden in all your shirt linings, huh?

MA: Here in "America"—losing is no problem. You know—End of the Year Bonus?

LONE: Oh, right.

MA: After I get that, I'll laugh at what I lost.

LONE: Lee told you there was a bonus, right?

MA: How'd you know?

LONE: When I arrived here, Lee told me there was a bonus, too.

MA: Lee teach you how to play?

LONE: Him? He talked to me a lot.

MA: Look, why don't you come down and start playing with the guys again?

LONE: "The guys."

MA: Before we start playing, Lee uses a stick to write "Kill!" in the dirt.

LONE: You seem to live for your nights with "the guys."

MA: What's life without friends, huh?

LONE: Well, why do *you* think I stopped playing?

MA: Hey, maybe you were the one getting killed, huh?

LONE: What?

MA: Hey, just kidding.

LONE: Who's getting killed here?

MA: Just a joke.

LONE: That's not a joke, it's blasphemy.

MA: Look, obviously you stopped playing 'cause you wanted to practice the opera.

LONE: Do you understand that discipline?

MA: But, I mean, you don't have to overdo it either. You don't have to treat 'em like dirt. I mean, who are you trying to impress?

(*Pause.* LONE *throws dice into the bushes.*)

Questions for Discussion

1. Why do you think Lone does not associate with the other men? Do you think this is a good thing? Why?

2. Ma is very naive. Is this believable? Why?

3. Ma and Lone are the only two characters in the play. They talk about the conditions under which the men have to live—yet Hwang never shows these conditions. Why do you think he wrote

the play this way? Would it be better to include other characters and to show how the adverse conditions affected them? Why or why not?

4. Under nearly hopeless conditions, Lone continues to practice his art. Why do you suppose this is so? Is it believable?

5. What is the significance of the game the two characters play?

Stanley Rosen: 16
Irving Yanover: 16
Length of scene: Three minutes and 15 seconds
to three minutes and 45 seconds

The Chopin Playoffs

Israel Horovitz/ *U.S.A.*

This is the final play in a trilogy about growing up as a Jew in a small Canadian town, Sault Sainte Marie, Ontario. The three plays are based on stories written by Morley Torgov, into which Horovitz weaves his own remembrances. Although Horovitz himself grew up in Wakefield, Massachusetts, the three plays first were presented on Canadian television and later adapted for the theatre.

The Chopin Playoffs, set in 1947, focuses on the intense piano-playing competition between Irving and Stanley, two high-school seniors. The one who wins will receive a college scholarship and, even more important, Fern's heart.

Fern has been dating both Stanley and Irving and at one point tells them that she can't tell them apart.

(STANLEY *moves downstage, talks as if on telephone*)

STANLEY: Yanover? I'm coming over. (*Lights fade up on an amazed* IRVING YANOVER, *in Yanover living room*)

IRVING: Who's this?

STANLEY: Stanley Rosen. (*The fight bell sounds as* STANLEY *crosses into the Yanover house*) She's nuts, you know. We don't look anything alike.

IRVING: Of course she's nuts. Nuts is the Human Condition. Have you read Camus?

STANLEY: (*Lying through his teeth*) Most of Camus. But it's been a long time.

IRVING: Uh hahhh! A blind spot in your intellectual growth, Rosen! Now that I know your weakness, I shall leap in and triumph . . .

STANLEY: I never saw two men look less alike!

IRVING: I agree.

(STANLEY *crosses to table*)

STANLEY: Do you think Fern's father is really a Nazi?

IRVING: Naw, I don't think he's so much a Nazi as he is a Nazi supporter.

STANLEY: Mmm. (*Nods in agreement*)

IRVING: It's exactly like you not being so much an athlete as an athletic supporter . . .

STANLEY: (*They both squeeze invisible horns and make "nahn-nah" sounds*) Ho, ho! *That* was rich. (*Pauses*) Could we leap over the small talk, up to some medium talk, Yanover?

IRVING: Be my guest: leap.

STANLEY: How'd you get your parents around the idea of Fern Fipps being somebody you date?

IRVING: Parents, my dear Rosen, have a strong tendency to see life *as they want it to be,* rather than life as it most obviously *is* . . . until, of course, a Stanley Rosen comes along and takes the truth and tries to *rub it in my parents' eyes!*

STANLEY: A basic survival technique, my dear Yanover. Blind the enemy parent with the truth and your own parents will never see the *truth* . . .

IRVING: If I were you, I wouldn't go into philosophy for a living . . .

STANLEY: You know what Plato said?

IRVING: Remind me.

STANLEY: Plato said, "Never wear argyle socks with a glen-plaid suit."

IRVING: Plato was in the menswear business?

STANLEY: "Morris Plato's Togary."

IRVING: Is it true what my father said? That you wrote a song called "Prelude to the Sale of a Pair of Pants"? That's what your father told *my* father, anyway . . .

STANLEY: I did. I did that.

IRVING: I composed a tune called "Fanfare for Five Flannel Sheets and a Pillowcase."

STANLEY: You ever play four-handed Gershwin?

IRVING: Is that like doubles pinochle?

STANLEY: Aha! A major blind spot! Do you know Oscar Levant?

IRVING: Didn't he live over on Pim Street?

STANLEY: Get serious, Yanover! Oscar Levant is just about the greatest mind in the twentieth century, that's all . . . He wrote a book called *A Smattering of Ignorance,* about how he and Gershwin fought all the time.

IRVING: They fought too, huh!

STANLEY: Oil and water . . . I'll loan you the book. It's just probably the greatest book every written in English, that's all.

IRVING: No kidding?

(STANLEY *produces a dog-eared copy of a book by Levant*)

STANLEY: *A Smattering of Ignorance.* Be my guest, Yanover. Just read the opening paragraph. (STANLEY *tosses book across store to* IRVING, *who catches it*) My life was changed by Oscar Levant. There's more to life than Frédéric Chopin, m'boy. (IRVING *is reading; pretends to be engrossed totally*)

IRVING: Shhh. I'm reading . . .

STANLEY: Some middlebrow would-be pseudointellectuals claim *Camus* has a brain, but history will prove that the *great* thinker of the twentieth century was, unquestionably, Oscar Levant . . .

IRVING: (*Looks up. Playacts exasperation*) Will you *please?* I am reading. If you think this is a good book, Rosen, you're out of your mind! This is a great book, Rosen! A Great Book!

STANLEY: I gave this book to my father to read.

IRVING: What did he say?

STANLEY: Obvious line: "I used to think you were a lunatic. Now I'm *convinced!*"

IRVING: Lunacy is a son's birthright . . .

STANLEY: It's in the Talmud. Page eight . . .

IRVING: Page *nine.*

STANLEY: You know your Talmud . . .

IRVING: Back to front . . .

STANLEY: Like the front of your hand . . .

IRVING: That was funny. Maybe I was Levant in an earlier life?

STANLEY: This is true, you were Levant and I was Gershwin. You see, my dear Yanover, the subtle difference between Levant and Gershwin is the subtle difference between talent and genius . . .

YANOVER: Really?

STANLEY: Really.

IRVING: You wanna try to back up your fancy talk with some fancy action?

STANLEY: Okay, palley-pal. You see these mitts? (*Makes two fists*)

IRVING: Yuh, so?

STANLEY: Watch 'em and weep. (STANLEY *walks to Irving's piano and plays Gershwin's* Rhapsody in Blue)

IRVING: That is just great, Rosen.

Questions for Discussion

1. Do you think it is logical for two high-school seniors to discuss philosophy the way Stanley and Irving do?

2. How do you think Irving and Stanley feel about each other? Use specific lines to back up what you say.

3. What provides the humor here? How would you go about getting this across to an audience?

4. Can you see any difference in the personalities of the two characters? Explain.

5. Can you identify with either or both of the boys? Explain. Do you care about them? Why?

Charley: 18 to 20
Jack: 18 to 20
Length of scene: 5:45 to 6:45 minutes

Charley's Aunt

Brandon Thomas/ *U.S.A.*

First presented in 1892, this play still is produced widely, most often by community theatres and schools. A delightful farce, it is about two college boys who dress a friend in women's clothing to play a rich aunt from Brazil. The reason for the deception is that the boys have invited two girls to their rooms for lunch—to meet the aunt, of course, who is delayed.

This scene occurs a minute or two into the play. Brassett, to whom Jack refers, is a servant. You may skip his line, if you wish.

CHARLEY (*mildly*): I say—! (*To center*)

JACK (*throwing down pen, jumping up savagely*): If you don't clear out, Brassett, I'll— (*Meets* CHARLEY *center.*) Oh, it's you, Charley! What is it, old chap?

CHARLEY: Nothing, Jack. I don't want to interrupt you if you're busy. (*Going.*)

JACK (*going center*): It's all right, Charley, don't go, it's only that fool Brassett.

CHARLEY: What's he doing? (*Coming back to center*)

JACK: Only bagging all my clothes because I'm going down, and worrying me like Old Harry while I'm trying to write a-most-important-letter. (*Moving towards table right*) Don't mind me to-day; I'm nervous and naggy and nonplussed. (*Sits on end of table right center*)

CHARLEY: And so am I, Jack.

JACK: Why?

CHARLEY: I've been trying to write a letter, too.

JACK: A letter! To whom?

CHARLEY: To—to Miss Spettigue.

JACK (*going to* CHARLEY, *center*): How far have you got?

(*Both center*)

CHARLEY (*brightening*): Oh! I began awfully well, but—I didn't want to be distant, and I didn't like to be too—too—

JACK: Familiar? Well?

CHARLEY: So I just said, "My Dear Amy"—and then words failed me, and I've come to you for advice. You always know what to say and do.

JACK (*dubiously, with a look towards letter*): Oh! Do I?

CHARLEY: You know my idiotic complaint; I'm shy—you're not.

JACK: Aren't I?

CHARLEY: So prescribe for me, old chap. What am I to say? (*Turning away left, sits right, corner of table center*)

JACK (*going right center, aside*): A good idea! I'll prescribe for him and take the medicine myself. (*Sits at writing-table right, gets paper, etc.*

Energetically.) Now then, let's see. You're in love with Amy Spettigue, and you want to know if there's any hope for you, and if so—

CHARLEY: You see, they're all off to Scotland tomorrow.

JACK: Yes, I know, and you want to see her at once. When and where?—bearer waits. Do I diagnose the case accurately?

CHARLEY: To a "Tee," old chap!

JACK: Very well then; you'll want to say something to this effect: (*writing*) "My Dear Kitty—" (*Stops dead*)

CHARLEY (*going to him, writing-table right center*): No—not Kitty— Amy.

JACK: Oh, of course, what am I thinking of? (*Tears up paper, takes fresh sheet. In casual, glib tone, writing.*) "My Dearest Amy— Forgive me, darling, for thus addressing you, but I love you so deeply"—under-lined—

CHARLEY (*surprised, moving nearer—interrupting*): Rather strong, Jack.

JACK: Shut up! "So earnestly"—also underlined—

CHARLEY: Oh, I say! (*Turning away center*)

JACK: "That I *must* write and tell you so. All I ask is—"

CHARLEY (*sits table center*): But there's one obstacle to my putting it quite as straight as that, much as I'd *like* to.

JACK: What's that?

CHARLEY: Well—er—I've an *aunt.*

JACK: My dear Charley, most of us have; what about her?

CHARLEY: I feel I ought to tell her first.

JACK (*flings down pen, rises and goes to fireplace*): Oh! If you're going to drag an *aunt* into the business, we may as well wait till they all come back from Scotland.

CHARLEY: Why?

JACK: You know what "auntie" is when *she* steps in.

CHARLEY: No, I don't. That's just it; I don't know her. I've never even *seen* her.

JACK: Well, we won't be too hard on that aunt; she hasn't interfered much in your affairs up to now.

CHARLEY: Except to find out that I was an orphan and have me sent to Eton, and to Oxford; and now my guardian writes to me that she's coming here this morning by an early train, and will take luncheon with me at one o'clock.

JACK (*coming down to back of chair left of writing table*): And you've never seen her?

CHARLEY: No. She went out to Brazil before I was born, and became a sort of secretary to a very rich old Brazilian chap out there, called Dom Pedro d'Alvadorez; and now—by the merest accident in the world (*taking "Truth" from pocket and pointing to marked paragraph*) I've seen this. (*Gives* JACK *paper.*)

JACK (*going down right. Note: "Lucia" is pronounced "LOOSIA"— Portuguese, NOT Spanish. Reading.*): "Madam—or rather Donna Lucia d'Alvadorez, the Brazilian millionaire, who has taken Lord Toppleby's magnificent mansion in Belgravia, is an English-woman of genial disposition, and a financial genius. Indeed, it was her capacity in this direction that earned the gratitude of her late husband, and led to a romantic deathbed marriage." (*To* CHARLEY.) Well, I don't see much in that! (*Offering paper back.*)

CHARLEY: Go on, Jack read the next.

JACK (*reading*): "Her only relation—is a nephew at Oxford"—lucky nephew!

CHARLEY: That's me.

JACK: By George, Charley, this is a starter! (*Throws paper to* CHARLEY.) And she may be here any minute? (*Goes to mantelpiece, looks at clock.*)

CHARLEY: I've met all the trains up to now. I wish she'd have come some other day. (*Rises, moves away down left a little.*)

JACK (*turning, looks at clock*): She'll arrive by the next, just in time for lunch.

CHARLEY (*dolefully*): Yes, it's a bore. I wanted to write that letter to Amy.

JACK (*sits on table right center, thinking*): I don't know so much about that!

CHARLEY (*comes center*): But it's an awfully difficult letter to write— fearfully complicated.

JACK: Why?

CHARLEY: Well, you see, I've no people or anything.

JACK: "No people," with an aunt like that! (*Pointing to paper which is in Charley's hand.*)

CHARLEY: But I've no reason to expect anything from her—more than she's already done for me—for which, of course, I'm very grateful and all that—but I was to see Amy and put it to her that if—

JACK (*suddenly—coming center to* CHARLEY): Charley! I've got a clinking good idea!

CHARLEY (*pushing* JACK *towards writing-table—gratefully*): Jack, you are a good chap! Write it down and I'll copy it out.

JACK (*stopping him*): No, not for you—for me—for us both. You're gone on Amy—I'm in love with Kitty.

CHARLEY: Really, Jack?

JACK: Madly. Worse than anything I ever took up—even cricket! I was writing to tell her so when you came in. (*Pointing.*) There's the letter.

CHARLEY (*wringing Jack's hand with effusion*): I'm so glad! and what's your "idea"?

JACK: Hang letter-writing! We'll give a luncheon party for your aunt, tea afterwards in the garden.

CHARLEY: In the garden?

JACK: Yes, I'll get leave.

CHARLEY: But my rooms are so small.

JACK: Never mind, I'll lend you mine. (*Pushing* CHARLEY *towards writing-table chair center.*) Brassett shall see to it. (*Calling towards left.*) Brassett! (*To* CHARLEY.) Now, come on! First we'll ask the girls.

CHARLEY: Ask the girls? (*Standing behind writing-table.*)

JACK (*by chair left of writing-table*): To meet your aunt.

CHARLEY: What about old Spettigue?

JACK: Blow old Spettigue!

CHARLEY: Oh, I forgot. He's up in town for a few days on business. (*Sits at writing-table.*)

JACK: So much the better. (*Calling.*) Brassett!

CHARLEY: Do you think they'll come?

JACK: They'll jump at it.

CHARLEY: What makes you think so?

JACK: Well, what do you think?

CHARLEY: Why, Jack, you know, I rather agree with you.

JACK: We'll send a note at once—you write it—go ahead.

(CHARLEY *writes to dictation.*)

"My Dear Miss Spettigue—" (*Calling.*) Brassett, where *are* you?

(BRASSETT, *left upper entrance, and comes down left of* JACK.)

Where *are* you? (*Turns, sees* BRASSETT *standing left*) Oh—er, Brassett, get someone to take a note to Mr. Spettigue's.

[BRASSETT: Yes, sir.]

(*Exits left.*)

CHARLEY: Yes, Jack, I've got that.

JACK (*gets envelope, pen and book to write on*): "Would you and Miss Verdun—" (*puts foot on chair left of writing-table and puts cigar-box on knee to write on*) "do me the honour—"

CHARLEY (*repeating*): —"the honour"—

JACK: —"to lunch with me and Mr. Chesney:"

CHARLEY (*repeating.*): —"Mr. Chesney"—

JACK: I'll address the envelope.

CHARLEY (*still repeating—while dipping pen in ink*): "I'll address the—"

JACK (*breaking in before* CHARLEY *can write it*): No, no that, you muff! "At his room, St. Olde's College, to-day at one o'clock." (*Addressing envelope.*) Miss Spettigue—

CHARLEY: Miss— (*about to write*).

(*Jack stops him before he writes.*)

JACK: No, look out! "To meet my aunt—" What did you say her name was, Charley?

CHARLEY: Donna Lucia d'Alvadorez.

JACK: "Donna"—All right, stick it down. "An answer by bearer will greatly oblige." (*Blots envelope.*)

CHARLEY (*writing*): "Yours sincerely. Charles Wykeham. (*Blots and folds letter.*) Splendid, Jack, you're a genius! (*Hands letter to* JACK.)

JACK (*takes letter, puts it in envelope and closes it*): It's a glorious opportunity. They're off to Scotland.

CHARLEY: And we're off "down."

JACK: And now we shall have them all to ourselves. (*Going left center*)

Questions for Discussion

1. Why do you suppose Jack is having trouble writing his own letter, but has no trouble at all dictating Charley's?

2. Is this scene believable? Can you relate to the situation? Explain.

3. Do you think Jack and Charley are typical college students of their day? Why?

4. Obviously, this scene is meant to be funny. Would you act out this scene differently than you would the scene from *The Chopin Playoffs*? What would you do differently? Why?

5. What does Charley mean when he says he has no "people"? Why is this important to him? Would this be as important in contemporary times? Explain.

Stanley: 12
Manny: 19
Length of scene: One minute and 30 seconds
to two minutes

A Rosen By Any Other Name

Israel Horovitz/ *U.S.A.*

This is the second play in the trilogy dealing with growing up as Jews in the small Canadian community of Sault Sainte Marie. But unlike *The Chapin Playoffs* (page 128), Horovitz writes that this play was "totally original, not found at all in Torgov's books." The play is set in 1941.

There are several themes at work in this play. It is near the beginning of World War II, and Stanley's father is afraid that Canada will begin to treat the Jews like Hitler does. So he decides he wants to change his name.

Stanley is about to have his Bar Mitzvah, and his mother, going overboard, wants to have a statue of him carved in chopped liver and photos of him on the napkins.

Manny Boxbaum, Stanley's cousin, has been discharged from fighting in World War II because he is shell-shocked. In this scene it is just after the morning he had a bad dream about being in the war and kept calling for a medic.

Stanley has called his girlfriend Fern to ask her if she'd go to Switzerland with him if Hitler invaded Canada. She has told him no. In the following scene, he turns this around.

STANLEY: Hey, Manny. You okay?

MANNY: Never better. I'm really sorry about last night.

STANLEY: That's okay. How shell-shocked are you, Manny?

MANNY: Pretty shell-shocked, I guess. . .

STANLEY: Shell-shocked is more scared than crazy, right?

MANNY: (*In unison with* STANLEY, *imitating* MANNY) You ain't just whistlin' "Dixie," m'boy!

STANLEY: (*Laughing*) I could see it on your face. You really looked scared.

MANNY: It comes and goes . . .

STANLEY: You don't look scared now.

MANNY: I'm not.

STANLEY: Good, 'cause I really need you to keep your promise to talk sense to my parents. I don't want to be selfish or anything. I mean, if you're still feeling shell-shocky or anything . . . don't feel you have to do me the favor, but if you're really feeling better and you think it won't upset you . . .

MANNY: (*Smiling*) Stanley, I'm O.K., really. . . . I'm a man of my word. I'll talk to your mother this morning . . .

STANLEY: Make your comments about the chopped-liver statue your own . . . I mean, don't tell her *I* hate it . . . let it be you who hates it, okay?

MANNY: How so?

STANLEY: If she thinks it's me who hates it, she'll close down her mind on the subject. But if she thinks it's you who hates it, she's liable to keep her own mind open . . . (*Pauses*) That's the way people are, Manny. It's exhausting, figuring these things out . . .

MANNY: I'll do the best I can, Stan, my man . . .

STANLEY: I know you will . . . I just hope your best is tough enough to wipe out her worst . . . I'm running out of time, Manny.

MANNY: I'll do my best . . . I'm sorry I scared you last night . . .

STANLEY: I wasn't scared. . . . The war's driving *everybody* crazy. I can tell. I was just talking with my girlfriend . . . Guess what she's after me to do . . .

MANNY: What?

STANLEY: Run away to Switzerland with her . . .

MANNY: You are joshing . . .

STANLEY: Not at all. Switzerland's not on either side, right?

MANNY: So they say . . .

STANLEY: Well, Fern's got it in her head to have us run away there . . .

MANNY: To elope?

STANLEY: Yeah, sort of.

MANNY: Before or after your Bar Mitzvah?

STANLEY: Are you kidding? My mother would gun us both down if we ran away before . . . What's "elope," exactly?

MANNY: Run away and get married . . .

STANLEY: Yuh, that's what I thought . . .

MANNY: Never ask the fruit salesman's daughter to run away with you and get married. You know why?

STANLEY: Why?

MANNY: She'll say she can't elope!

Questions for Discussion

1. Barney, Stanley's father, is convinced the Nazis will take over Canada. This is what spurred Stanley into asking Fern to go to Switzerland with him. Do you think Barney and Stanley have a right to be worried about Canada turning against the Jews? Explain.

2. Why do you think Stanley wants so much to have Manny talk to his mother about the chopped liver statue?

3. How do you think Stanley feels about Manny? What makes you think so?

4. What kind of a person do you think Manny is? Why? How does he feel about Stanley?

5. Stanley is very outspoken for a 12-year old. To what do you attribute his precociousness?

Scenes for
Three Actors

Steve: 18 to 20
Dale: 18 to 20
Grace: 18 to 20
Length of scene: Eleven minutes to twelve
minutes and 30 seconds

FOB

David Henry Hwang/ *U.S.A.*

The initials that make up this title mean "fresh off the boat." It is a three-character play, in which there are two Chinese American characters and one who has just arrived from China.

Basically, the play asks the question: What good do Chinese myths do for people living in America? This is the author's first play, initially produced in 1979 at Stanford University and in 1980 in New York. The action occurs in the back room of a Chinese restaurant in Torrance, California.

This scene is near the beginning of Act II. As the play opens, Steve speaks only a Chinese language. Gradually, his speech and understanding improve. He represents the person who believes in mythology, arguing with Chinese American people who no longer do, or at least have doubts about it.

The three characters have eaten dinner together at the restaurant. This scene occurs just afterward.

STEVE: Quiet! Do you know who I am?

DALE: Yeah—you're a FOB. You're a rich FOB in the U.S. But you better watch yourself. 'Cause you can be sent back.

STEVE: Shut up! Do you know who I am?

DALE: You can be sent back, you know—just like that. 'Cause you're a guest here, understand?

STEVE: (*To* GRACE) Tell him who I am.

DALE: I know who he is—heir to a fortune in junk merchandise. Big deal. Like being heir to Captain Crunch.

STEVE: Tell him!

(*Silence.*)

GRACE: You know it's not like that.

STEVE: Tell him!

DALE: Huh?

GRACE: All the stuff about rice bowls and—zippers—have you ever been there, Dale?

DALE: Well, yeah. Once. When I was ten.

GRACE: Well, it's changed a lot.

DALE: Remember getting heat rashes.

GRACE: People are dressing really well now—and the whole place has become really stylish—well, certainly not everybody, but the people who are well-off enough to send their kids to American colleges— they're really kinda classy.

DALE: Yeah.

GRACE: Sort of.

DALE: You mean, like him. So what? It's easy to be classy when you're rich.

GRACE: All I'm saying is . . .

DALE: Hell, I could do that.

GRACE: Huh?

DALE: I could be classy, too, if I was rich.

GRACE: You *are* rich.

DALE: No. Just upper-middle. Maybe.

GRACE: Compared to us, you're rich.

DALE: No, not really. And especially not compared to him. Besides, when I was born we were still poor.

GRACE: Well, you're rich now.

DALE: Used to get one Life Saver a day.

GRACE: That's all? One Life Saver?

DALE: Well, I mean, that's not all I lived on. We got normal food, too.

GRACE: I know, but . . .

DALE: Not like we were living in cardboard boxes or anything.

GRACE: All I'm saying is that the people who are coming in now—a lot of them are different—they're already real Westernized. They don't act like they're fresh off the boat.

DALE: Maybe. But they're still FOBs.

STEVE: Tell him who I am!

DALE: Anyway, real nice dinner, Grace. I really enjoyed it.

GRACE: Thank you.

STEVE: Okay! I will tell myself.

DALE: Go tell yourself—just don't bother us.

GRACE: (*Standing, to* STEVE) What would you like to do now?

STEVE: Huh?

GRACE: You wanted to go out after dinner?

STEVE: Yes, yes. We go out.

DALE: I'll drive. You sent the hearse home.

STEVE: I tell driver—return car after dinner.

DALE: How could you . . . ? What time did you . . . ? When did you tell him to return? What time?

STEVE: (*Looks at his watch*) Seven-five.

DALE: No—not what time is it. What time you tell him to return?

STEVE: Seven-five. Go see.

(DALE *exits through kitchen.*)

STEVE: (*No accent*) Why wouldn't you tell him who I am?

GRACE: Can Gwan Gung die?

(*Pause.*)

STEVE: No warrior can defeat Gwan Gung.

GRACE: Does Gwan Gung fear ghosts?

STEVE: Gwan Gung fears no ghosts.

GRACE: Ghosts of warriors?

STEVE: No warrior ghosts.

GRACE: Ghosts that avenge?

STEVE: No avenging ghosts.

GRACE: Ghosts forced into exile?

STEVE: No exiled ghosts.

GRACE: Ghosts that wait?

(*Pause.*)

STEVE: (*Quietly*) May I . . . take you out tonight? Maybe not tonight, but some other time? Another time? (*He strokes her hair.*) What has happened?

DALE: (*Entering*) I cannot believe it . . . (*He sees them.*) What do you think you're doing? (*He grabs* STEVE'*s hand. To* STEVE) What . . . I step out for one second and you just go and—hell, you FOBs are sneaky. No wonder they check you so close at Immigration.

GRACE: Dale, I can really take care of myself.

DALE: Yeah? What was his hand doing, then?

GRACE: Stroking my hair.

DALE: Well, yeah. I could see that, I mean, what was it doing stroking your hair? (*Pause*) Uh, never mind. All I'm saying is . . . (*He gropes.*) Jesus! If you want to be alone, why don't you just say so, huh? If that's what you really want, just say it, okay?

(*Pause.*)

DALE: Okay. Time's up.

GRACE: Was the car out there?

DALE: Huh? Yeah. Yeah, it was. I could not believe it. I go outside and—thank God—there's no limousine. Just as I'm about to come back, I hear this sound like the roar of death and this big black shadow scrapes up beside me. I could not believe it!

STEVE: Car return—seven-five.

DALE: And when I asked him—I asked the driver, what time he'd been told to return. And he just looks at me and says, "Now."

STEVE: We go out?

DALE: What's going on here? What is this?

STEVE: Time to go.

DALE: No! Not till you explain what's going on.

STEVE: (*To* GRACE) You now want to dance?

DALE: (*To* GRACE) Do you understand this? Was this coincidence?

STEVE: (*Ditto*) I am told good things of American discos.

DALE: (*Ditto*) You and him just wanna go off by yourselves?

STEVE: I hear of Dillon's.

DALE: Is that it?

STEVE: You hear of Dillon's?

DALE: It's okay, you know.

STEVE: In Westwood.

DALE: I don't mind.

STEVE: Three—four stories.

DALE: Really.

STEVE: Live band.

DALE: Cousin.

STEVE: We go.

(*He takes* GRACE'*s hand.*)

DALE: He's just out to snake you, you know. (*He takes the other hand. From this point on, almost unnoticeably, the lights begin to dim.*)

GRACE: Okay! That's enough! (*She pulls away.*) That's enough! I have to make all the decisions around here, don't I? When I leave it up to you two, the only place we go is in circles.

DALE: Well . . .

STEVE: No, I am suggesting place to go.

GRACE: Look, Dale, when I asked you here, what did I say we were going to do?

DALE: Uh—dinner and a movie—or something. But it was a different "we," then.

GRACE: It doesn't matter. That's what we're going to do.

DALE: I'll drive.

STEVE: My car can take us to movie.

GRACE: I think we better not drive at all. We'll stay right here. (*She removes* STEVE's *tie.*) Do you remember this?

DALE: What—you think I borrow clothes or something? Hell, I don't even wear ties.

(GRACE *takes the tie, wraps it around* DALE's *face like a blindfold.*)

DALE: Grace, what are you . . . ?

GRACE: (*To* STEVE) Do you remember this?

DALE: I already told you. I don't need a closer look or nothing.

STEVE: Yes.

GRACE: (*Ties the blindfold, releases it*) Let's sit down.

DALE: Wait.

STEVE: You want me to sit here?

DALE: Grace, is he understanding you?

GRACE: Have you ever played Group Story?

STEVE: Yes, I have played that.

DALE: There—there he goes again! Grace, I'm gonna take . . .

(*He starts to remove the blindfold.*)

GRACE: (*Stopping him*) Dale, listen or you won't understand.

DALE: But how come *he's* understanding?

GRACE: Because he's listening.

DALE: But . . .

GRACE: Now, let's play Group Story.

DALE: Not again. Grace, that's only good when you're stoned.

GRACE: Who wants to start? Steve, you know the rules?

STEVE: Yes—I understand.

DALE: See, we're talking normal speed—and he still understood.

GRACE: Dale, would you like to start?

DALE: All right. (*By this time, the lights have dimmed, throwing shadows on the stage.* GRACE *will strike two pots together to indicate each speaker change and the ritual will gradually take on elements of Chinese opera.*) Uh, once upon a time . . . there were . . . three bears—Grace, this is ridiculous!

GRACE: Tell a story.

DALE: . . . three bears and they each had . . . cancer of the lymph nodes. Uh—and they were very sad. So the baby bear said, "I'll go to the new Cedar Sinai Hospital, where they may have a cure for this fatal illness."

GRACE: But the new Cedar Sinai Hospital happened to be two thousand miles away—across the ocean.

STEVE: (*Gradually losing his accent*) That is very far.

DALE: How did—? So, the bear tried to swim over, but his leg got chewed off by alligators—are there alligators in the Pacific Ocean?—Oh, well. So he ended up having to go for a leg *and* a cure for malignant cancer of the lymph nodes.

GRACE: When he arrived there, he came face to face with—

STEVE: With Gwan Gung, god of warriors, writers, and prostitutes.

DALE: And Gwan Gung looked at the bear and said . . .

GRACE: . . . strongly and with spirit . . .

STEVE: "One-legged bear, what are you doing on my land? You are from America, are you not?"

DALE: And the bear said, "Yes. Yes."

GRACE: And Gwan Gung replied . . .

STEVE: (*Getting up*) By stepping forward, sword drawn, ready to wound, not kill, not end it so soon. To draw it out, play it, taunt it, make it feel like a dog.

DALE: Which is probably rather closely related to the bear.

GRACE: Gwan Gung said—

STEVE: "When I came to America, did you lick my wounds? When I came to America, did you cure my sickness?"

DALE: And just as Gwan Gung was about to strike—

GRACE: There arrived Fa Mu Lan, the Woman Warrior. (*She stands, faces* STEVE. *From here on in, striking pots together is not needed.*) "Gwan Gung."

STEVE: "What do you want? Don't interfere! Don't forget, I have gone before you into battle many times."

DALE: But Fa Mu Lan seemed not hear Gwan Gung's warning. She stood between him and the bear, drawing out her own sword.

GRACE: "You will learn I cannot forget. I don't forget, Gwan Gung. Spare the bear and I will present gifts."

STEVE: "Very well. He is hardly worth killing."

DALE: And the bear hopped off. Fa Mu Lan pulled a parcel from beneath her gown. (*She removes* DALE*'s blindfold.*)

DALE: She pulled out two items.

GRACE: "This is for you." (*She hands blindfold to* STEVE.)

STEVE: "What is that?"

DALE: She showed him a beautiful piece of red silk, thick enough to be opaque, yet so light, he barely felt it in his hands.

GRACE: "Do you remember this?"

STEVE: "Why, yes. I used this silk for sport one day. How did you get hold of it?"

DALE: Then she presented him with a second item. It was a fabric—thick and dried and brittle.

GRACE: "Do you remember this?"

STEVE: (*Turning away*) "No, no. I've never seen this before in my life. This has nothing to do with me. What is it—a dragon skin?"

DALE: Fa Mu Lan handed it to Gwan Gung.

GRACE: "Never mind. Use it—as a tablecloth. As a favor to me."

STEVE: "It's much too hard and brittle. But, to show you my graciousness in receiving—I will use it tonight!

DALE: That night, Gwan Gung had a large banquet, at which there was plenty, even for the slaves. But Fa Mu Lan ate nothing. She waited until midnight, till Gwan Gung and the gods were full of wine and empty of sense. Sneaking behind him, she pulled out of the tablecloth, waving it above her head.

GRACE: (*Ripping the tablecloth from the table*) "Gwan Gung, you foolish boy. This thing you have used tonight as a tablecloth—it is the stretched and dried skins of my fathers. My fathers, whom you slew—for sport! And you have been eating their sins—you ate them!"

STEVE: "No. I was blindfolded. I did not know."

DALE: Fa Mu Lan waved the skin before Gwan Gung's face. It smelled suddenly of death.

GRACE: "Remember the day you played? Remember? Well, eat that day, Gwan Gung."

STEVE: "I am not responsible. No. No." (GRACE *throws one end of the tablecloth to* DALE, *who catches it. Together, they become like* STEVE's *parents. They chase him about the stage, waving the tablecloth like a net.*)

DALE: Yes!

GRACE: Yes!

STEVE: No!

DALE: You must!

GRACE: Go!

STEVE: Where?

DALE: To America!

GRACE: To work!

STEVE: Why?

DALE: Because!

GRACE: We need!

STEVE: No!

DALE: Why?

GRACE: Go.

STEVE: Hard!

DALE: So?

GRACE: Need.

STEVE: Far!

DALE: So?

GRACE: Need!

STEVE: Safe!

DALE: Here?

GRACE: No!

STEVE: Why?

DALE: Them.

(*Points.*)

GRACE: Them.

(*Points.*)

STEVE: Won't!

DALE: go!

GRACE: Go!

STEVE: Won't!

DALE: Must!

GRACE: Must!

STEVE: Won't!

DALE: Bye!

GRACE: Bye!

STEVE: Won't!

DALE: Fare!

GRACE: Well!

> (DALE *and* GRACE *drop the tablecloth over* STEVE, *who sinks to the floor.* GRACE *then moves offstage, into the bathroom–storage room, while* DALE *goes upstage and stands with his back to the audience. Silence.*)

STEVE: (*Begins pounding the ground*) Noooo! (*He throws off the table-cloth, standing up full. Lights up full, blindingly.*) I am GWAN GUNG!

DALE: (*Turning downstage suddenly*) What . . . ?

STEVE: I HAVE COME TO THIS LAND TO STUDY!

DALE: Grace . . .

STEVE: TO STUDY THE ARTS OF WAR, OF LITERATURE, OF RIGHTEOUSNESS!

DALE: A movie's fine.

STEVE: I FOUGHT THE WARS OF THE THREE KINGDOMS!

DALE: An ordinary movie, let's go.

STEVE: I FOUGHT WITH THE FIRST PIONEERS, THE FIRST
WARRIORS THAT CHOSE TO FOLLOW THE WHITE
GHOSTS TO THIS LAND!

DALE: You can pick, okay?

STEVE: I WAS THEIR HERO, THEIR LEADER, THEIR FIRE!

DALE: I'll even let him drive, how's that?

STEVE: AND THIS LAND IS MINE! IT HAS NO RIGHT TO
TREAT ME THIS WAY!

GRACE: No. Gwan Gung, *you* have no rights.

STEVE: Who's speaking?

GRACE: (*Enters with a* da dao *and* mao, *two swords*) It is Fa Mu Lan.
You are in a new land, Gwan Gung.

STEVE: Not new—I have been here before, many times. This time, I
said I will have it easy. I will come as no ChinaMan before—on a
plane, with money and rank.

GRACE: And?

STEVE: And—there is no change. I am still treated like this! This
land . . . has no right. I AM GWAN GUNG!

GRACE: And I am Fa Mu Lan.

DALE: I'll be Chiang Kai-shek, how's that?

STEVE: (*To* DALE) You! How can you—? I came over with your parents.

GRACE: (*Turning to* STEVE) We are in America. And we have a battle to
fight. (*She tosses the* da dao *to* STEVE. *They square off.*)

STEVE: I don't want to fight you.

GRACE: You killed my family.

STEVE: You were revenged—I ate your father's sins.

GRACE: That's not revenge!

(*Swords strike.*)

GRACE: That was only the tease.

(*Strike.*)

GRACE: What's the point in dying if you don't know the cause of your death?

(*Series of strikes.* Steve *falls.*)

DALE: Okay! That's it!

(GRACE *stands over* STEVE, *her sword pointed at his heart.* DALE *snatches the sword from her hands. She does not move.*

DALE: Jesus! Enough is enough!

(DALE *takes* STEVE*'s sword; he also does not react.*)

DALE: What the hell kind of movie was that?

(DALE *turns his back on the couple, heads for the bathroom–storage room.* GRACE *uses her now-invisible sword to thrust in and out of* STEVE*'s heart once.*)

DALE: That's it. Game's over. Now just sit down here. Breathe. One. Two. One. Two. Air. Good stuff. Glad they made it. Right, cousin?

Questions for Discussion

1. Do you feel that ethnic culture should be preserved? Why?

2. What was the significance of the "game" the three characters played?

3. Consider how Steve moved from speaking and understanding little English to handling the language very well. Did he lose anything in the process?

4. Each of the three characters represents a different facet of Chinese society in America. Can you see what each is? Explain.

5. What is the significance of the argument that went on for a time after Steve's line, "I am not responsible. No. No."?

Jack: 18 to 20
Lord Fancourt: 18 to 20
Charley: 18 to 20
Length of scene: Six minutes to seven minutes

Charley's Aunt

Brandon Thomas/*U.S.A.*

Jack and Charley have decided to have a luncheon and invite their girlfriends, but Brassett tells them that their credit is exhausted, so they cannot buy food. Finally, Brassett agrees to charge things in his name. The two boys then decide to ask Lord Fancourt, whom they call Fanny Babbs (his real name is Fancourt Babberly) to meet Charley's aunt and bring her to the luncheon. They figure he can entertain her while they spend time with their girlfriends.

In this scene, they try to talk him into it.

JACK (*comes down right, to* LORD FANCOURT, *center*): I looked you up last night, Babbs, but you were out.

(CHARLEY *comes down left*)

LORD FANCOURT (*center*): Yes. You know Freddy Peel, don't you? He's an awful idiot—hasn't a particle of brains, has he? But *I'm* all right! He gave a card party last night, and I won a hundred pounds from him. You should have seen his face! It makes me laugh now.

JACK: Why, Freddy Peel hasn't sixpence!

LORD FANCOURT: No, really?

CHARLEY: Did he pay you?

LORD FANCOURT: No, but he's going to—when his grandmother dies.

JACK: Why, the old lady's been dead years!

LORD FANCOURT: No, really? That's beastly! You know, I'm stumped, and he's had an awful lot out of me. But he's an awful idiot, hasn't a particle of brains, has he? But I'm all right! (*Picks up bag*) Ta-ta; I'm off! (*Attempts to bolt towards window.*)

(JACK *intercepts and brings him back to table as before.* JACK *puts bag on table.*)

JACK (*down right*): I say, Babbs, we want you to stay and lunch with us to-day.

LORD FANCOURT (*center*): I say, you chaps, don't play the giddy goat! I've got to meet my tutor.

JACK (*with mock concern*): Babbs, you mustn't work like this. You're looking quite pulled down.

LORD FANCOURT (*to* JACK): Am I really? (*Turns to* CHARLEY.)

CHARLEY: I was only telling Jack so just now.

LORD FANCOURT: Do you think I shall die? (*Turns to* JACK.)

JACK: Not you! You don't want to worry over all this study. You'll be a great man of one sort or the other one of these days without all that.

LORD FANCOURT: Well, that's what *I* think, you know. But I ought to do something. We've had a wonderful lot of Johnnies in our family—great Johnnies in the army and navy and things!

JACK: I'll bet they never killed themselves with study!

LORD FANCOURT: No, but I must do *something*.

JACK: Of course, Babbs, you must stay to lunch. Charley's aunt is going to pay him a visit.

LORD FANCOURT: No, really? What fun! I know Charley visits his "uncle" sometimes, when he's hard up (*pulling* CHARLEY'*s watch out by the chain*), so it's only right his aunt should return the visit.

(*All laugh, pushing* LORD FANCOURT *to and fro.* CHARLEY *regains his watch.*)

JACK: Now that's just the sort of thing we want—a jolly smart chap like you, with a fund of humour and a lot of brilliant conversation. (*Turns* LORD FANCOURT *round so that they face each other.*)

CHARLEY: Yes, Babbs, that's it! (*Hands on* LORD FANCOURT'*s shoulders and turns him round same as* JACK *has done, so that they face each other.*)

JACK (*pulls him back facing center*): To interest and amuse a charming lady.

LORD FANCOURT: Yes. Who is she?

JACK: Why, Charley's Aunt.

LORD FANCOURT: What's she like?

CHARLEY: Well, you see, Babbs, we don't quite know. I'm to see her to-day for the first time.

LORD FANCOURT: I say, Charley, she may turn out to be an awful old "croc."

JACK: She's a widow, and a millionaire, that's enough, isn't it?

LORD FANCOURT: Rather! (*To* CHARLEY.) Put me down for a chance, Charley. I'll take a chance!

JACK: We didn't care to ask Freddy Peel, did we, Charley?

CHARLEY: No. (*Turning away left*)

JACK: No.

LORD FANCOURT: No. He's an awful idiot!—I say, what's her name?

CHARLEY (*deliberately*): Donna Lucia d'Alvadorez.

LORD FANCOURT: Oh, dem it, what a name! (*Seizes bag again and bolts to door left*)

(JACK *and* CHARLEY *bring him back, right center, turn him round and run him up to table center on which he falls face downwards, putting bag on table. Jack brings him down center again.*)

JACK: Look here, Babbs, it's no use; you must stay to lunch. You'll find Charley's Aunt a *charming* old lady.

LORD FANCOURT: Charming *old* lady! I say, look here, haven't you got anything younger coming?

CHARLEY: Oh yes, two other ladies.

LORD FANCOURT: Nice? Young?

CHARLEY: Yes.

LORD FANCOURT: Ah! That's more in my line. How many did you say?

JACK: Two.

LORD FANCOURT: Oh, I see. One for each of you, and the old "croc" for me. No thanks, I'm off!

(LORD FANCOURT *bolts up right of table center towards window with his bag and is brought back as before.*)

JACK (*coming down right of him*): Now listen Babbs. This is an awfully serious affair.

LORD FANCOURT (*center*): I should think so, with an old "croc" like that!

CHARLEY (*coming down left of him*): And we want your *help* as a friend.

JACK: Yes, Babbs, a friends we can *trust*, eh?

LORD FANCOURT: Rather!

JACK: We'll take you into our confidence. No humbug—straight as a die. We're in love.

LORD FANCOURT: What, Charley as well? You silly ass! (*Pushes him away, sits on table center*)

(CHARLEY *goes down left*)

JACK: No fool of a flirtation business, but the real downright serious thing. (*Sits on corner of writing-table.*)

CHARLEY: And Babbs, if you knew the girls as well as we do, you wouldn't wonder at it.

JACK: And they're coming here to lunch to-day.

LORD FANCOURT: I say, have you proposed? (*From one to the other.*)

JACK: No, that's just it.

LORD FANCOURT: Oh, I see. You want me to propose for you?

JACK: *No!* We'll do that for ourselves. That's why we've asked them to come.

CHARLEY: You know, Babbs, you don't understand our feelings a bit.

LORD FANCOURT: Oh, don't I, though. I say—(*Rises, comes down center, beckons boys to him. All center*) Haven't you noticed how sad I've been lately?

CHARLEY: Yes.

JACK: What is it?

LORD FANCOURT: Well, I don't know, but I think—I'm in love too.

CHARLEY: What makes you think that?

LORD FANCOURT: I'm always wanting to be alone, and hear the birds sing.

(JACK *and* CHARLEY *laugh.*)

And I'm getting so fond of poetry. I can't sleep. I took to drink for a couple of days, but it made me ill for a week, so I left it off.

JACK: You've got all the symptoms. Sit down and tell us all about it.

(LORD FANCOURT *goes to chair right of table center.* CHARLEY *sits on table center.* JACK *sits at table right.* LORD FANCOURT *places his hat on* CHARLEY*'s foot.* CHARLEY *removes it.*)

LORD FANCOURT: You remember when I was ploughed?

JACK: Beastly shame!

LORD FANCOURT: No, not last time—the term before. I was awfully ill, and took the yacht round to the Mediterranean, and at Monte Carlo I came across an English officer named Delahay—quite penniless and dying. You know, Jack, he tried to commit suicide.

JACK: Bad luck at the tables, eh?

LORD FANCOURT: Yes. He'd beggared himself and his only child, the sweetest girl you ever saw, Jack. And to amuse him and keep his spirits up, I used to play cards with him.

CHARLEY: And what became of him?

LORD FANCOURT: He died, poor fellow!

JACK: And what became of her—the sweetest little girl you ever saw?

LORD FANCOURT: I lost sight of her. A lady travelling home that way— from South America, I believe—took charge of her and brought her to England. You know, Jack, I tried to tell her that—

JACK: You loved her?

LORD FANCOURT: But she was in such grief that—

JACK: It all oozed out of your finger-tips and the points of your hair!

LORD FANCOURT: But after all, you know, I might have been rejected and I should have looked a silly ass.

JACK: At any rate, you can sympathise with us.

(*Knock off left*)

(*Enter* BRASSETT *left and exits left*)

JACK: Hallo! Here's the messenger back.

(JACK, LORD FANCOURT *and* CHARLEY *all hurry across left.* BRASSETT *re-enters with note, hands it to* JACK *and goes up left center to sideboard, quietly arranges three tumblers, whiskey decanter and jug of water on tray during next scene.*)

(*Opens letter and reads.*) They're coming!

(*They are looking over each other's shoulders while* JACK *opens note.* LORD FANCOURT *takes note from* JACK.)

LORD FANCOURT: By Jove!

(CHARLEY *takes it from him.* LORD FANCOURT *is left staring at his thumb and two first fingers spread out.*)

CHARLEY: So they are! (*Goes right and sits in writing-chair with his back to* JACK *and* LORD FANCOURT, *reading letter.*)

JACK: You'll stop, Babbs?

LORD FANCOURT: Oh, I say—look here—(*Looks at clothes.*)

JACK: No, you'll do as you are. We won't let you go now we've got you.

LORD FANCOURT: But look here, Jack, don't play the giddy goat; I've something else to do.

JACK: What is it?

LORD FANCOURT: It's something awfully important.

JACK: Well, what?

LORD FANCOURT: I'm going to play in some amateur theatricals.

JACK: Rot! He'll be ploughed again—won't he, Charley?

LORD FANCOURT: But I've given my word.

JACK: What are you playing?

LORD FANCOURT: A lady—an old lady—and I've never acted in my life before—

JACK: Oh! That's his tutor, eh, Charley?

LORD FANCOURT: And I'm going to try on the things before those fellows come.

JACK: You can try them on here. Where are they?

LORD FANCOURT: In my rooms, in a box on the bed, but—

Questions for Discussion

1. What role does exaggeration play in this scene?

2. What part, if any, do emotions or feelings play in this scene?

3. How would you describe Lord Fancourt—his looks and personality? How would you describe Jack? Charley?

4. Why do you think this play has retained its popularity for more than 100 years?

5. If you were choosing the next production for a school or community theatre, would you consider *Charley's Aunt?* Why or why not?

Libby: 15 to 17
Liz: 15 to 17
Beth: 15 to 17
Length of scene: Seven minutes and 15 seconds
to eight minutes and 15 seconds

Fables for Friends

Mark O'Donnell/ *U.S.A.*

This play is complete in itself, and was one of nine plays presented during the mid-1980s at Playwrights Horizons in New York City. All nine of the plays dealt with important points in the lives of the characters—turning points, changes, or rites of passage that everyone goes through on the way to adulthood.

This scene takes places just after three high-school girls have stopped off at a diner. They become more and more uncomfortable as they feel they are being watched by an older man.

(*Three* P.M.: *A diner. The three girls enter energetically.*)

LIZ: I could have died!

BETH: I could have died too!

LIBBY: I missed it.

BETH: Let's all order the same thing. Hi, Tony!

LIZ (*to the unseen Tony*): We're fine.

BETH: I danced with Brian Culver on Sadie Hawkins night; he's a very sincere dancer.

LIBBY: He held the water fountain faucet for me once, after he'd had his drink.

BETH: Libby, you are too wonderful. (*Then, to* LIZ) But even if you are his confidante, big whoop! Who needs that?

LIZ: Things happen. I'm not gonna eat, are you?

BETH: Are you?

LIZ: If you are.

LIBBY: I can make something at home for free. I can use the blender or anything.

BETH: Libby, you are too wonderful.

LIBBY: Beth, would you open your mouth on the very first kiss?

LIZ (*intruding*): With a certain boy?

LIBBY: Yeah. Or in a certain life.

LIZ: Well, if he sincerely likes you—

LIBBY: What if he says he likes you, does that mean he does?

LIZ (*simultaneously with* BETH): Yes.

BETH (*simultaneously with* LIZ): No. (*Under such contradiction, they quickly reverse their stands and contradict each other simultaneously again.*)

LIZ: No.

BETH: Yes.

LIZ (*to settle it*): Assume it's yes, you'll get more done.

BETH (*swiftly*): Let's all order the same thing. That way they'll be no fighting once it comes. Yes? Three yeses? We'll all have the same thing like we were sisters eating at home.

LIZ: What if we all order the same thing and when it comes it's gross? I would die, that would be the end.

LIBBY: Yes, let's order different things. We can feed each other off our own plates.

LIZ: This is weird, there's a milk stain on the table from my ice water glass.

BETH: It's from the people before you. I'm going to have the burger plate. Maybe my zillionth one is free.

LIZ: The weirdest thing has been happening to me—

BETH: Like what, like that? Big whoop.

LIBBY: Are you all already to order?

LIZ: Yeah, I'll have the Brian Culver, no toast.

BETH: You wish. Oh, he's here. The burger plate. Amen.

LIZ: Yes, I'll have the—uh—slice of pizza plain—I forget is that with cheese? And a *cola*. (*She laughs at the term.*)

BETH (*playing along*): Oh, and a *cola* for me too.

LIBBY: Me too. Oh, is it my turn? And a donut.

BETH: No make that your *diet cola*.

LIZ (*thrilled by the implicit mockery*): For me too!

LIBBY: Me too! (*They watch the waiter go, and laugh simultaneously.*)

BETH: We're all having the same *beverage!*

LIZ (*imitating a nasal robot*) *Beverage! Beverage* with your *meal!* (*Laughter*)

LIBBY: We sure are having a good time, huh? (*This casts a pall on the proceedings. Then, to re-spark the conversation*) I love your new jacket, Liz. It's old, huh?

LIZ: Are you kidding? West Tech burned down ten years ago, I'd be going to a vacant lot!

BETH: What a goof! Liz the varsity quarterback.

LIZ: I found it in the Salvation Army.

BETH: It's so funny. I love the dumb colors, red and white.

LIZ: Look at this "Skipper." If only they could have seen themselves back in those days.

LIBBY: Did they have anything green? I've decided I'm going to wear only green from now on so I can have an image.

LIZ: Wait'll you see, I bought somebody's old wedding picture, too. I'm going to hang it in my locker. My mother is so confused— She asked if I *knew* the people! Right, as if I were around in the nineteen thirties! (*Pause*) I'm gonna marry Tony and eat here for free.

LIBBY: We could eat here forever!

BETH: One thing I could not marry is that jukebox. It's slow, it is, it plays "I'll Never Tell You" slow somehow, and that song demands not a slow rhythm.

LIZ: Maybe the little men inside are tired of playing it for you.

LIBBY: Boy, it's a good thing we're nuts, huh! (*Another pall is cast.*) It helps to be nuts like us! (*Silence.* BETH *begins to hum "I'll Never Tell You." No recognizable tune emerges.*)

BETH (*joined by* LIBBY): I'll never tell you, no, no, no, . . . See? It demands to be fast. (LIZ *has frozen, unnnoticed by* BETH.) Remember that record album I played for you over the phone last week?

LIZ (*intensely*): Sssh!

BETH: What?

LIZ: Shht! Everybody just act natural.

BETH: What's the matter?

LIZ: Nothing, everything is normal, don't turn your head.

LIBBY: If everything is normal, why do we have to act natural?

LIZ: Because that man over there is looking at us!

BETH: What!

LIZ: He's been staring at us!

LIBBY (*over-imagining the danger*): Oh my God, and, please, angels—

LIZ (*sharply*): Libby—

BETH: This is too weird. I'm sorry.

LIZ: He's looking. Don't look! (LIBBY *shuts her eyes.*) You can open your eyes, Libby, I mean don't look at *him*. Look how old he is! Don't look! At the counter.

LIBBY (*not looking*): Oh my God!

BETH: Oh my water! (*Intentionally spills her ice water.*) Sorry, Libby, we better clean this up! (*She raises an unnatural fuss that allows her to steal looks at the counter.*) Napkins, napkins, here, let's shake off. Oopsy daisy!

LIBBY: It's fine, water doesn't stain.

BETH (*in a fake, loud voice*): Thank goodness, huh! Thank goodness it doesn't stain! This is nice, did you get this at Peddler's Cove? I often go there! Sit. (*To* LIZ) I can't believe how old he is.

LIZ: I know, but he's not that old.

BETH: Some of his—I could see some gray hairs.

LIBBY: Is he kind of distinguished old, like he might have an important job?

LIZ: Come on, he's in Tony's.

LIBBY: Maybe he's from some place foreign, where they look at each other.

LIZ: The stories you make up for people would make for a world of real dips.

BETH: He does look safe, though, not crazy.

LIZ: Are you trying to marry me to this guy?

BETH: He's staring at *you,* Liz.

LIBBY (*scared*): Don't be scared, Liz!

LIZ: With my luck he's some gross uncle I was introduced to and forgot.

BETH: Have you ever had to handle a crush before?

LIZ (*She hasn't*): Well of course. Of course I have. You're not around me every second. But this guy is so old. I can't tell him he'll find someone else.

LIBBY: Don't look back at him!

LIZ: I have to do something!

LIBBY (*"Think of your career"*): You could be head of Debating Club next year!

LIZ: Let's not jump the gun here—

BETH: Don't do anything! What are you going to do?

LIZ: Okay. Tony has to bring the cokes. That'll be like something that happens.

LIBBY (*frightened*): Then we tell Tony?

LIZ: I'll get up as if to stretch—and go find out what he wants.

LIBBY: Liz, don't talk to him!

BETH (*significantly: "D-Day"*): Here are the cokes. (*They sit up painfully straight as the cokes are supposedly distributed. They watch Tony go.*)

LIBBY (*determined not to see him*): Is he having coke?

LIZ (*peeking at the man*): He's having coffee.

BETH (*factually*): Gross.

LIZ: I'll ask to borrow the sugar.

LIBBY: Oh my God.

LIZ: Come on, it's four o'clock in the afternoon! (*They unwittingly exchange aviators' chocks-away glances. LIZ makes an unlikely stretch and goes.*) Geronimo!

BETH: Liz! (*To LIBBY, herself excited but trying to be calming*) Okay, okay now.

LIBBY: Okay, okay.

BETH: She's out of her mind!

LIBBY: Why are you grinning?

BETH: I can't help it. This isn't fun, I promise. Don't look! Is she talking to him?

LIBBY: No, he's talking to her, I can hear him. (*Both close their eyes and clasp hands, as if on a roller coaster.*)

BETH: Is that your heart or mine?

LIBBY: I don't know. (*Pause*) I wish I could save her.

BETH: Why did you ask before about if someone likes you? Does somebody *like* you?

LIBBY: No.

BETH: Who?

LIBBY: Terry Glauber. (*Pause. She lends an ear.*) Still talking.

BETH: He *should* like you, you're better than him.

LIBBY: He's supposed to stay in the hospital for another two months. Maybe then it would work out.

BETH: Oh, don't worry. I'm sure it'll be better than I think it'll be. (*Pause. Then, as an excuse to turn around.*) Tony! This isn't *diet* soda!

LIBBY: Don't turn around!

BETH: Are you trying to murder me by overweight? Ha-ha!

LIBBY: What are you doing?

BETH: The guy is writing something for her. His address!

LIBBY: Is she crazy? Does he know how old she isn't? I bet she told him she was her older sister. (*Pause. Sips her drink.*) This is *so* diet coke, it tastes like ashes.

BETH: I needed a reason to—shh, here she comes. Come on, act like yourself. (*Silence.* LIZ *returns, sits, dazed. Silence.*)

LIBBY: Hi.

BETH: There's your coke.

LIBBY: Are you okay?

BETH: The guy's leaving. He's going. Liz—

LIBBY (*absurdly, since* LIZ *is very still*): Let her catch her breath.

LIZ (*finally*): The jacket belonged to his son.

BETH: Jacket? Your jacket? What about— Wasn't he watching you?

LIBBY: Are you all right?

LIZ: He saw the Skipper. This.

BETH: He thinks his son wants his letter jacket back? After ten years?

LIZ: No.

BETH: That's all he wanted, his son's jacket?

LIZ: His son was killed in a car crash. (*Awful silence, though not too long*)

LIBBY: Without the jacket?

BETH: Yes, without the jacket, sshh.

LIBBY: Oh, Liz.

LIZ: Some girl must have had it. He must've given it to some girl to wear who gave it to the Salvation Army eventually.

LIBBY: The dad didn't know who? (LIZ *shakes her head.*) Maybe she had to. Maybe she got married.

BETH: Are you giving it back?

LIZ (*nods*): He was afraid I'd get cold. He said I should wear it home.

BETH: Oh. (*They all contemplate this opportunity briefly.*)

LIBBY: He did seem nice. (*Pause*) Though I never saw him. (*Pause*)

BETH: Oh, here's the food, uh, yes. (*Indicating* LIZ) That was her—I was the burger plate.

LIBBY: I was the donut.

Questions for Discussion

1. Do you think the three girls are typical high-school students? Why?

2. If something like this happened to you, how do you think it would affect you? Why?

3. Do you think the encounter with the father of the boy killed in the crash would have a lasting effect on Liz? Explain.

4. Do you think the situation portrayed here is believable or realistic? Why?

5. What thoughts do you think are going through the girls' heads as they see the man watching them? Explain.

Hero: 18 to 20
Margaret: 18 to 22
Beatrice: 18 to 20
Length of scene: Two minutes and 40 seconds
to three minutes and 20 seconds

Much Ado About Nothing

William Shakespeare/*England*

Claudio, a young lord of Florence, has returned from war and is deeply in love with Hero, daughter of the governor of Messina. Don Pedro offers to help Claudio by impersonating him at a masquerade and wooing Hero for him. A servant mishears and reports that Don Pedro, the prince—rather than Claudio—is in love with Hero. Don John, Don Pedro's corrupt brother, leads Claudio to believe the untruth. Things are eventually set right, and a wedding is planned. But it cannot be completed short of a week.

Don Pedro suggests in the meantime that Claudio and Hero pass the week trying to make Benedick, a young lord, and Beatrice, the governor's niece, fall in love. At the same time, Don John plots to break up the match between Claudio and Hero.

In Act III, scene iv, Hero is in her apartment, preparing for her wedding along with Ursula and Margaret, her attendants, and Beatrice, her cousin. When you present the scene, if you wish, you can simply pause to acknowledge responses from Ursula or you can include a fourth actress.

HERO: Good Ursula, wake my cousin Beatrice and desire her to rise.

[URSULA: I will, lady.]

HERO: And bid her come hither.

[URSULA: Well.]   (*Exit.*)

MARGARET: Troth, I think your other rebato[1] were better.

HERO: No, pray thee, good Meg, I'll wear this.

MARGARET: By my troth's not so good, and I warrant your cousin will say so.

HERO: My cousin's a fool, and thou art another. I'll wear none but this.

MARGARET: I like the new tire[2] within excellently, if the hair were a thought browner, and your gown's a most rare fashion, i' faith. I saw the Duchess of Milan's gown that they praise so.

HERO: Oh, that exceeds, they say.

MARGARET: By my troth, 's but a nightgown[3] in respect of yours,— cloth o' gold, and cuts,[4] and laced with silver, set with pearls, down sleeves, side sleeves,[5] and skirts round underborne[6] with a bluish tinsel. But for a fine, quaint, graceful, and excellent fashion, yours is worth ten on 't.

HERO: God give me joy to wear it! For my heart is exceeding heavy.

MARGARET: 'Twill be heavier soon by the weight of a man.

HERO: Fie upon thee! Art not ashamed?

MARGARET: Of what, lady? Of speaking honorably? Is not marriage honorable in a beggar? Is not your lord honorable without marriage? I think you would have me say, "saving your reverence,[7] a husband." An bad thinking do not wrest true speaking, I'll offend nobody. Is there any harm in "the heavier for a husband"? None, I think, an

---

[1] high collar or frame of wire that supports the ruff

[2] headdress

[3] dressing gown; house coat

[4] places where the original material has been cut away to show the fabric underneath.

[5] Down sleeves hang to the waist; side sleeves hang from the shoulder.

[6] worn over

[7] an apology for an improper word or remark

it be the right husband and the right wife; otherwise 'tis light, and not heavy. Ask my Lady Beatrice else—here she comes.

(*Enter* BEATRICE.)

HERO: Good morrow, coz.

BEATRICE: Good morrow, sweet Hero.

HERO: Why, how now? Do you speak in the sick tune?[8]

BEATRICE: I am out of all other tune, methinks.

MARGARET: Clap 's into "Light-o'-love."[9] That goes without a burden.[10] Do you sing it, and I'll dance it.

BEATRICE: Ye light-o'-love, with your heels! Then, if your husband have stables enough, you'll see he shall lack no barns.[11]

MARGARET: Oh, illegitimate construction! I scorn that with my heels.

BEATRICE: 'Tis almost five o'clock, Cousin, 'tis time you were ready. By my troth, I am exceeding ill. Heigh-ho!

MARGARET: For a hawk, a horse, or a husband?

BEATRICE: For the letter that begins them all, H.[12]

MARGARET: Well, an you be not turned Turk,[13] there's no more sailing by the star.

BEATRICE: What means the fool, trow?[14]

MARGARET: Nothing I, but God send everyone their heart's desire!

HERO: These gloves the Count sent me. They are an excellent perfume.

BEATRICE: I am stuffed,[15] Cousin, I cannot smell.

MARGARET: A maid, and stuffed! There's goodly catching of cold.

BEATRICE: Oh, God help me! God help me! How long have you professed apprehension?[16]

---

[8] as if you do not feel well

[9] begin singing "Light-o'-love," a well-known song in Elizabethan times

[10] chorus

[11] This is a pun on the word *bairns,* meaning children.

[12] In Elizabethan times "H" and "ache" were homonyms.

[13] become a heathen

[14] I wonder.

[15] I have a cold.

MARGARET: Ever since you left it. Doth not my wit become me rarely?

BEATRICE: It is not seen enough, you should wear it in your cap. By my troth, I am sick.

MARGARET: Get you some of this distilled *Carduus Benedictus*[17] and lay it to your heart. It is the only thing for a qualm.[18]

HERO: There thou prickest her with a thistle.

BEATRICE: *Benedictus?* Why *Benedictus?* You have some moral[19] in this *Benedictus.*

MARGARET: Moral! No, by my troth, I have no moral meaning, I meant plain holy thistle. You may think perchance that I think you are in love. Nay, by 'r Lady, I am not such a fool to think what I list; nor I list not to think what I can; no, indeed, I cannot think, if I would think my heart out of thinking, that you are in love, or that you will be in love, or that you can be in love. Yet Benedick was such another, and now is he become a man. He swore he would never marry, and yet now, in despite of his heart, he eats his meat without grudging. And how you may be converted, I know not, but methinks you look with your eyes as other women do.

BEATRICE: What pace is this that thy tongue keeps?

Margaret: Not a false gallop.[20]

(*Re-enter* URSULA.)

[URSULA: Madam, withdraw. The Prince, the Count, Signior Benedick, Don John, and all the gallants of the town, are come to fetch you to church.]

HERO: Help to dress me, good coz, good Meg, good Ursula.

(*Exeunt.*)

---

[16] quick wit

[17] Literally, this means blessed thistle. It refers to an herb that often was thought to cure a variety of ailments.

[18] feeling ill

[19] a hidden meaning

[20] canter

Questions for Discussion

1. How do Hero, Margaret, and Beatrice differ in their views of marriage?

2. There are a number of puns in this scene. Point out and explain what they are.

3. Why do you think Margaret keeps changing what she says about how Hero looks or should look?

4. Why do you think Margaret tries to talk Beatrice into marrying Benedick?

5. Hero, of course, is getting ready to go to the church for her wedding. Do you think the dialogue in this scene is appropriate for such an occasion? Explain.

Scenes for Multiple Actors

Death by Stages

As You Like It

Campfire

West Side Story

Will: 21	Robeson: 21
Chekhov: 18	Garrick: 18
Helen Hayes: 22	Wayne: 24
Sarah Bernhardt: 19	Gielgud: 14
Nell: 17	

Length of scene: Three minutes and 30 seconds to four minutes and 30 seconds

Death by Stages

Zachary Thomas/ *U.S.A.*

The play is set 200 years in the future. A nuclear holocaust, coupled with genetic experimentation, has pretty much set the world back to what it was like in Elizabethan England.

Now genetic engineering has been forbidden except for actors, who are compelled to take potions that change them so that they physically become their roles. Also, they have no choice whether they wish to become actors—they are chosen as young children. Worst of all, the potions wreak such havoc with their bodies that they rarely live beyond the age of 25 or so. Some opt for suicide because of all the pain the changes cause. The actors also are compelled to choose names of well-known performers throughout history. Will is William Shakespeare; Nell is Nell Gwynn; Wayne is John Wayne; and so on.

Colley Cibber is different because his body will not change, yet he wants to be an actor. Many of the others, however, suspect he is behind what happened to Marilyn Monroe. After the evening's performance, she takes the potion to regain her own physical body and can't change back. She races from the theatre in near hysterics, vowing to find whoever was responsible.

(*Everyone is seated at a large round table in an Elizabethan-style inn as* WILL *and* NELL *enter.*)

WILL: I see you haven't been served yet.

CHEKHOV: Any word about Marilyn?

(HELEN HAYES *and* SARAH BERNHARDT *scoot their chairs around to make room.* WILL *holds a chair for* NELL. *She sits down and so does* WILL.)

ROBESON: Is Marilyn all right?

NELL: It would seem so. But we can't be certain.

CHEKHOV: What do you mean?

NELL: She wasn't at her lodging.

HELEN: It's a darned shame.

CHEKHOV: How could this happen? The formulas have worked for a hundred years.

ROBESON: Have they?

GARRICK: I don't follow your meaning. I think their development was a wonder. A boon for all of us who would tread the boards.

BERNHARDT: Perhaps. Nevertheless, we have little to look forward to beyond the gaslights and makeup.

CHEKHOV: I, for one, think the man who developed the formulas should rot in hell through all eternity for what he's done.

WILL: Parsons Dowd?

CHEKHOV: That's right.

GARRICK: I disagree. If it weren't for the theatre, my mum and my brothers and sister would be turned out in the streets by now.

CHEKHOV: There is that. But it seems to me—

ROBESON: It seems to me that we have big trouble on our hands. (*He looks from face to face.*) Things have gone strangely awry the past few days.

HELEN: The formula's gone bad, is that what you mean?

ROBESON: I for one don't think it's the formulas.

CHEKHOV: Nor I.

BERNHARDT: Are you implying it's deliberate? That someone's behind it?

CHEKHOV: Figure it out for yourself. Never in the history of the theatre has this thing happened.

ROBESON: Or so we're led to believe.

WILL: You're right. There's no way of knowing.

ROBESON: I suspect someone's deilberately altering the formulas.

WILL: But who? And for what purpose?

BERNHARDT: I can think of one person.

WILL: I've had my suspicions too. But I have nothing to base them on.

GARRICK: Of course, you mean Cibber. (*He looks* WILL *straight in the eyes, a seeming taunt behind the words.*)

WILL: (*Irritated*) Because he can't alter his body?

GIELGUD: I understand Richard Burbage took the poison. Well before his years.

WAYNE: Don't worry none, laddie. Your time ain't coming for awhile yet.

(GIELGUD *gives* WAYNE *a dirty look.*)

CHEKHOV: So I assume that most of us suspect some sort of foul play.

(*The others murmur assent.*)

CHEKHOV: So what are we going to do?

WILL: (*Glancing at* NELL) Nell, are you all right?

NELL: As much as anyone can be in times like these. What's to be done?

ROBESON: You said you couldn't find Marilyn. Where do you suppose she'd gone?

WILL: (*Pulling a note from his pocket*) This is all she said. (*He hands the paper to* HELEN *who glances at it and then passes it around the table.*) What about it , Nell? Did she say anything before she ran off? Anything that would give you a clue?

NELL: No. (*She frowns.*) Yes. Yes, she did. She shouted something to Smitley about getting the guilty person.

WILL: What did she mean? Do you think she suspected someone?

NELL: (*Shaking her head*) Who could she have suspected? Who would do such a terrible thing?

CHEKHOV: Who do you think? You get two guesses and the second doesn't count.

BERNHARDT: Cibber, of course. Who else?

WILL: I can't imagine he'd do such a terrible thing. And what would be his motive?

GARRICK: Jealousy. He wants to be one of us and can't be. Isn't that plain?

NELL: But to do something so extreme. No, I never liked the man, but I don't see how he'd be capable of doing something like this.

ROBESON: Where is he tonight, by the way? It's not like him to miss out on dinner.

(GARRICK *snickers.*)

ROBESON: (*Giving him a piercing look*) I didn't mean to imply that the man shouldn't eat.

GARRICK: Isn't it obvious that's who Marilyn went to see?

WILL: But why?

BERNHARDT: Maybe Garrick's right. I've always thought it a little strange that Cibber never could change. Especially when he wants to be one of us.

CHEKHOV: They tell me that a lot of youngsters used to be stagestruck. They dreamed of careers in the theatre. In fact, the man whose name I took wrote lessons for this sort of person. I think Cibber's like one of those youngsters. The theatre means so much to him that I . . . well, I just can't see him doing anything to hurt it or anyone in it.

WAYNE: It's interesting. Some of us had other ambitions, would give anything not to be actors. And then someone like Cibber is just the opposite. He apparently would sell his soul to be able to change.

HELEN: Didn't there used to be a saying about the grass always being greener somewhere else?

GIELGUD: I like the company and all. But if I could, I'd rather be doing other work. This wouldn't have been my choice.

WAYNE: And what would you rather be doing? Raising brats or raising chickens?

GARRICK: I've always been interested in carpentry and in building.

WAYNE: (*Laughing derisively*) Do you liken yourself to our Lord?

WILL: Leave the boy be. Most of us have other dreams, lives that might have been.

ROBESON: These are serious times. We shouldn't bicker but must stick together.

Questions for Discussion

1. Which of the characters do you feel is the most sympathetic? Who is the least sympathetic? Why?

2. How would you feel about acting if you were a member of this troupe?

3. Why do you suppose some of the other actors suspect that Cibber is behind what happened to Marilyn?

4. Why do you suppose Wayne baits John Gielgud, embarrassing him in front of the others?

5. What do you think is the most appropriate single adjective you could apply to each of these characters? Why?

Rosalind: About 18
Orlando: About 20 or 21
Phebe: About 18
Silvius: About 20 or 22
Length of scene: One minutes and 45 seconds
to two minutes and 15 seconds

As You Like It

William Shakespeare/*England*

This scene from Act V takes place in the forest where Rosalind, still disguised as a boy calling herself Ganymede, has met Orlando. He is unhappy because Celia and Oliver (Orlando's brother) will marry the next day, and he still has not found Rosalind. "Ganymede" promises to produce her the following day.

Phebe, in love with Ganymede, enters, followed by Silvius, who loves her. Phebe rebukes Rosalind for showing Silvius a love letter Phebe wrote to Ganymede.

[ROSALIND]: Look, here comes a lover of mine and a lover of hers.

PHEBE (*to* ROSALIND):
Youth, you have done me much ungentleness,[1]
To show the letter that I writ to you.

ROSALIND:
I care not if I have. It is my study[2]
To seem despiteful and ungentle to you.
You are there followed by a faithful shepherd.
Look upon him; love him. He worships you.

PHEBE (*to* SILVIUS):
Good shepherd, tell this youth what 'tis to love.

SILVIUS:
It is to be all made of sighs and tears;
And so am I for Phebe.

PHEBE: And I for Ganymede.

ORLANDO: And I for Rosalind.

ROSALIND: And I for no woman.

SILVIUS:
It is to be all made of faith and service;
And so am I for Phebe.

PHEBE: And I for Ganymede.

ORLANDO: And I for Rosalind.

ROSALIND: And I for no woman.

SILVIUS:
It is to be all made of fantasy,[3]
All made of passion and all made of wishes,
All adoration, duty, and observance,
All humbleness, all patience and impatience,
All purity, all trial,[4] all observance;[5]
And so am I for Phebe.

---

[1]discourteous

[2]specific purpose

[3]imagination

[4]enduring any trial

[5]devotion

PHEBE: And so am I for Ganymede.

ORLANDO: And so am I for Rosalind.

ROSALIND: And so am I for no woman.

PHEBE (*to* ROSALIND):
    If this be so, why blame you me to love you?

SILVIUS (*to* PHEBE):
    If this be so, why blame you me to love you?

ORLANDO:
    If this be so, why blame you me to love you?

ROSALIND: Why do you speak too, "Why blame you me to love you?"

ORLANDO: To her that is not here, nor doth not hear.

ROSALIND: Pray you, no more of this; 'tis like the howling of Irish
    wolves against the moon. (*To* SILVIUS.) I will help you, if I can.
    (*To* PHEBE.) I would love you, if I could.—Tomorrow meet me all
    together. (*To* PHEBE.) I will marry you, if ever I marry woman, and
    I'll be married tomorrow. (*To* SILVIUS.) I will content you, if what
    pleases you contents you, and you shall be married tomorrow.
    (*To* ORLANDO.) As you love Rosalind, meet. (*To* ORLANDO.) I will
    satisfy you, if ever I satisfied man and you shalt be married
    tomorrow.(*To* SILVIUS.) As you love Phebe, meet. And as I love no
    woman, I'll meet. So fare you well.   I have left you commands.

SILVIUS: I'll not fail, if I live.

PHEBE: Nor I.

ORLANDO: Nor I.

    Exeunt (separately).

Questions for Discussion

1. Why do you suppose Rosalind persists in pretending she's
   Ganymede?

2. Where is the humor in this scene? If you were in the audience,
   would you find this scene funny? Why or why not?

3. What do you think of Silvius' definition of love? Do you agree with
   him?

4. Rosalind is confident that she will cause Phebe to marry Silvius and to make everyone happy with her. How then would you describe her views about marriage? Are they realistic?

5. What emotions would you try to portray if you were portraying each of the characters in this scene?

Ogg: 14 (male)	Ugg: 11 (female)
Oog: 15 (male)	Igg: 22 (male)

Various other men, women, children of the tribe
Length of scene: Two minutes to ?

Campfire

Marsh Cassady/ *U.S.A.*

The following play is more like an acting game and is mostly just for fun. Of course, it is to be done largely in pantomime, using nonsense language. The hunt can be as long or as short as you want to make it, as involved or as simple. There can be any number of characters beyond the four mentioned.

Ogg and Oog are young hunters. Ugg is Ogg's wife, and Igg is chief of the tribe. The action occurs in the Pleistocene era, many thousands of years B.C. People have learned to live together as clans and tribes but have not yet developed a verbal language. It is just after a long hunt. The entire tribe sits around a big fire. They've all had a hard day of hunting and being hunted. Everyone is dressed in animal skins. As the scene begins, all the characters sit staring into the flames while dinner cooks on a spit.

OGG: (*Suddenly jumping to his feet*) Ooo, uuh, ooo, uuh. uuh. (OGG *looks at the others, waiting for their reactions. All of them turn to face* OGG, *puzzled looks on their ape-like faces.*)

OOG: Inga, inga inga. Uuk, uuk. (*He taps a finger against his temple and points to* OGG *as if to say: "You're crazy, man. We don't behave like this in a social gathering."*)

OGG: (*Shaking his head in anger*) Ooga, ooda, odda!

UGG: (*Glancing from* OGG *to* OOG) Poo, poo, poo, patowy.

IGG: (*Spreading his hands, palms outward in a gesture indicating the others should be quiet*) Sooda, sawda. (*He nods onces and points toward* OGG.)

OGG: (*Baring his teeth in what must be a smile*) Katuch, katuch, ick-ick. (*Everyone now watches intently to see what* OGG *will do.* OGG *walks inside the circle, just far enough from the fire so his legs won't be scorched. He picks up his bow, which had been lying beside his wife* UGG. *He pulls an imaginary arrow from the skin quiver on his back, crouches and sneaks around the entire circle. The he motions to* OOG *and* IGG *to join him. They do, all crouching now, slowly circling the fire. Suddenly* OOG *stops, the others nearly bumping into him. He sights off into the distance, motions the others to follow. Suddenly, he raises his bow, aims and shoots his imaginary arrow.* OGG *and* IGG *do the same with the bows. Suddenly, they race around the circle.* UGG *kneels, draws a sharp flint stone from his belt and slices the neck of an imaginary animal. Then he and the other two slit the imaginary belly, and pantomime dragging the creature back to the campfire, all of them laughing, slapping each other's backs and making strange verbal sounds of excitement. Grins on their faces, they look at the other tribe members, who are laughing and jabbering excitedly.*)

Questions for Discussion

1. Do you think this is how acting started? Why?

2. Besides having fun, what could be other reasons for presenting a scene such as this?

3. Although all the characters are young, they are responsible people. They have to be—anyone reaching the age of 26 or 27 is considered ancient. How would you portray this feeling that you are young but weighed down with the problems of survival?

4. This is the first scene in a loosely structured play about life in prehistoric times. What other scenes do you think would be logical to include? Try to improvise some of them, using just the basic idea.

5. Do you enjoy this sort of acting where more is required of you in establishing the dialogue and action? Why or why not?

Anybodys: Between 15 and 18 (female) **Baby John:** Between 15 and 18 (male)
Action: Between 15 and 18 (male) **A-rab:** Between 15 and 18 (male)
Diesel: Between 15 and 18 (male) **Anita:** Between 15 and 18 (female)
Snowboy: Between 15 and 18 (male)
Length of scene: Three minutes and 30 seconds to four minutes

West Side Story

Arthur Laurents/ *U.S.A.*

The play is a modern retelling of Shakespeare's tragic love story *Romeo and Juliet* with the boy (Tony) and the girl (Maria) on opposite sides of warring gangs in New York City, instead of feuding families in Verona.

The following scene is a combination of cuttings from Act One (Scenes 2 and 4) of *West Side Story,* which was first performed as a musical in 1957 with music by Leonard Bernstein and lyrics by Stephen Sondheim. Set in an alley, this scene begins with the Jets learning that the Sharks—a Puerto Rican rival gang—have found out about Tony and Maria and that Chino, friend of Bernardo, who is the leader of the Jets, is threatening to "get" Tony. Later, in Doc's drugstore, Anita appears and tries to get a warning to Tony. The Jets don't trust her; after all, she is Bernardo's girlfriend.

ANYBODYS: Buddy boys!

ACTION: Ah! Go wear a skirt.

ANYBODYS: I got scabby knees. Listen—

ACTION: (*to the gang*) Come on, we got make sure those PRs [Puerto Ricans] know we're on top.

DIESEL: Geez, Action, ain't we had enough?

ANYBODYS: (*going after them*) Wotta buncha Old Man Rivers: they don't know nothin' and they don't say nuthin'.

ACTION: Diesel, the question ain't whether we had enough—

ANYBODYS: The question is: Where's Tony and what party is lookin' for him.

ACTION: What do you know?

ANYBODYS: I know I gotta get a skirt. (*She starts off, but* DIESEL *stops her.*)

DIESEL: Come on, Anybodys, tell me.

SNOWBOY: Ah, what's the freak know?

ANYBODYS: Plenty. I figgered somebody oughta infiltrate PR territory and spy around. I'm very big with shadows, ya know. I can slip in and out of 'em like wind through a fence.

SNOWBOY: Boy, is she ever makin' the most of it!

ANYBODYS: You bet your fat A, I am!

ACTION: Go on. Wadd'ya hear?

ANYBODYS: I heard Chino tellin' the Sharks somethin' about Tony and Bernardo's sister. And then Chino said, "If it's the last thing I do, I'm going to get Tony."

ACTION: What'd I tell ya? Them PRs won't stop!

SNOWBOY: Easy, Action!

DIESEL: It's bad enough now—

BABY JOHN: Yeah!

ACTION: You forgettin'? Tony came through for us Jets. We gotta find him and protect him from Chino.

A-RAB: Right!

ACTION: OK then! Snowboy—cover the river! (SNOWBOY *runs off.*)

A-rab—get over to Doc's.

BABY JOHN: I'll take the back alleys.

ACTION: Diesel?

DIESEL: I'll cover the park.

ACTION: Good boy! (*He begins to run off.*)

ANYBODYS: What about me?

ACTION: You? You get a hold of the girls and send 'em out as liaison runners so we'll know who's found Tony where.

ANYBODYS: Right! (*She starts to run off.*)

ACTION: Hey! (*She stops.*) You done good, buddy boy.

ANYBODYS: (*she has fallen in love*) Thanks, Daddy-o.

(*They both run off.*)

• ———————— •

11:40 p.m. The drugstore.

A-RAB *and some of the Jets are there as* ANYBODYS *and other Jets run in.*

ACTION: Where's Tony?

A-RAB: Down in the cellar with Doc.

DIESEL: Ya warn him about Chino?

A-RAB: Doc said he'd tell him.

BABY JOHN: What's he hidin' in the cellar from?

SNOWBOY: Maybe he can't run as fast as you.

ACTION: Cut the frabbajabba.

ANYBODYS: Yeah! The cops'll get hip, if Chino and the PRs don't.

ACTION: Grab some readin' matter; play the juke. Some of ya get outside and if ya see Chino or any PR—

(*The shop doorbell tinkles as* ANITA *enters. Cold silence, then slowly she comes down to the counter. They all stare at her. A long moment. Someone turns on the jukebox; a mambo[1] comes on softly.*)

ANITA: I'd like to see Doc.

ACTION: He ain't here.

———————

[1] the music for a dance of Cuban origin

ANITA: Where is he?

A-RAB: He's gone to the bank. There was an error in his favor.

ANITA: The banks are closed at night. Where is he?

A-RAB: You know how skinny Doc is. He slipped in through the night-deposit slot.

ANYBODYS: And got stuck halfway in.

ACTION: Which indicates there's no tellin' when he'll be back. *Buenas noches, señorita.*

(ANITA *starts to go toward the cellar door.*)

DIESEL: Where you goin'?

ANITA: Downstairs—to see Doc.

ACTION: Didn't I tell ya he ain't here?

ANITA: I'd like to see for myself.

ACTION: (*nastily*) Please.

ANITA: (*controlling herself*) . . . Please.

ACTION: *Por favor.*²

ANITA: Will you let me pass?

SNOWBOY: She's too dark to pass.

ANITA: (*low*) Don't.

ACTION: *Please* don't.

SNOWBOY: *Por favor.*

DIESEL: *Non comprende.*³

A-RAB: *Gracias.*⁴

BABY JOHN: *Di nada.*⁵

ANYBODYS: Ai! Mambo! Ai!

ANITA: Listen, you— (*She controls herself.*)

ACTION: We're listenin'.

---

²(Sp.) Please.

³(Sp.) I don't understand. (A misuse of *no comprendo*)

⁴(Sp.) Thank you.

⁵(Sp.) You're welcome. (A misuse of *de nada*)

ANITA: I've got to give a friend of yours a message. I've got to tell Tony—

DIESEL: He ain't here.

ANITA: I know he is.

ACTION: Who says he is?

A-RAB: Who's the message from?

ANITA: Never mind.

ACTION: Couldn't be from Chino, could it?

ANITA: I want to stop Chino! I want to help!

ANYBODYS: Bernardo's girl wants ta help?

ACTION: Even a greaseball's got feelings.

ANYBODYS: But she wants to help get Tony!

ANITA: No!

ACTION: Not much—Bernardo's tramp!

SNOWBOY: Bernardo's pig!

ACTION: Ya lyin' Spic—!

ANITA: Don't do that!

BABY JOHN: Gold tooth!

DIESEL: Pierced ear!

A-RAB: Garlic mouth!

ACTION: Spic! Lyin' Spic!

(*The taunting breaks out into a wild, savage dance, with epithets hurled at* ANITA, *who is encircled and driven by the whole pack. At the peak, she is shoved so that she falls in a corner.* BABY JOHN *is lifted up high and dropped on her as* DOC *enters from the cellar door and yells.*)

Questions for Discussion

1. Do you think these two scenes are reasonable portrayals of gang life? Why?

2. What do you suppose causes gang rivalries such as this one?

3. Do you think it logical that the girlfriend of a gang leader would go into rival territory? Why?

4. From its first production, *West Side Story* has remained popular. What do you think accounts for that popularity?

5. Do you think threre is a legitimate comparison between Romeo and Juliet's love story and Tony and Maria's? Why?

Performance Information Chart

TITLE	ROLE	AGE	APPROXIMATE TIME

Scenes for One Male and One Female

TITLE	ROLE	AGE	APPROXIMATE TIME
The Stonewater Rapture	Whitney	18	3:30–4:30
	Carlyle	18	
Secret Service	Wilfred	16	4:30–5:30
	Caroline	15–16	
The Way of the World	Millamant	18	5:15–6:15
	Mirabell	20–22	
The Wrong Man	Nadia	?	3:00–3:30
	John	?	
End of Summer	Paula	20	4:30–5:30
	Will	20–21	
My Friend Never Said Goodbye	Annie	15–20	5:30–6:30
	Tommie	15–20	
Joe Turner's Come and Gone	Zonia	11	6:00–7:00
	Reuben	11	
Goat Song	Stanja	20	2:45–3:15
	Mirko	20s	
The Merchant of Venice	Portia	18–22	8:15–10:15
	Bassanio	20s	

Scenes for Two Females

TITLE	ROLE	AGE	APPROXIMATE TIME
My Sister in This House	Christine	20	2:45–3:15
	Lea	17–19	
Antigone	Antigone	18–20	5:45–6:45
	Ismene	20s	
Twelfth Night	Olivia	18–20	3:30–4:00
	Viola	18–20	
Shadow of a Man	Lupe	12	2:15–2:45
	Leticia	17	

Scenes for Two Females (continued)

TITLE	ROLE	AGE	APPROXIMATE TIME
Album	Peggy	14	2:30–3:00
	Trish	14	
As You Like It	Celia	18	3:45–4:15
	Rosalind	18	

Scenes for Two Males

TITLE	ROLE	AGE	APPROXIMATE TIME
Scars	Bob	18	3:00–3:45
	Timothy	17	
Two Gentlemen of Verona	Valentine	18–20	3:00–3:30
	Proteus	18–20	
Enter Laughing	David	18	4:45–5:45
	Marvin	18	
Winterset	Carr	17	5:15–6:15
	Mio	17	
Brighton Beach Memoirs	Eugene	15	4:30–5:30
	Stan	18½	
The Dance and the Railroad	Lone	20	5:15–6:15
	Ma	18	
The Chopin Playoffs	Stanley	16	3:15–3:45
	Irving	16	
Charley's Aunt	Charley	18–20	5:45–6:45
	Jack	18–20	
A Rosen by Any Other Name	Stanley	12	1:30–2:00
	Manny	19	

Scenes for Three Actors

TITLE	ROLE	AGE	APPROXIMATE TIME
FOB	Steve	18–20	11:00–12:30
	Dale	18–20	
	Grace	18–20	
Charley's Aunt	Jack	18–20	6:00–7:00
	Fancourt	18–20	
	Charley	18–20	
Fables for Friends	Libby	15–17	7:15–8:15
	Liz	15–17	
	Beth	15–17	

Scenes for Three Actors (continued)

TITLE	ROLE	AGE	APPROXIMATE TIME
Much Ado about Nothing	Hero	18–20	2:40–3:20
	Margaret	18–22	
	Beatrice	18–20	

Scenes for Multiple Actors

TITLE	ROLE	AGE	APPROXIMATE TIME
Death by Stages	Will	21	3:30–4:30
	Chekhov	18	
	Helen	22	
	Sarah	19	
	Nell	17	
	Robeson	21	
	Garrick	18	
	Wayne	24	
	Gielgud	14	
As You Like It	Rosalind	18	1:45–2:15
	Orlando	20–21	
	Phebe	18	
	Silvius	20–22	
Campfire	Ogg	14	2:00–?
	Oog	15	
	Ugg	11	
	Igg	22	
	Others	10–21	
West Side Story	Anybodys	15–18	3:30–4:00
	Action	15–18	
	Diesel	15–18	
	Snowboy	15–18	
	Baby John	15–18	
	A-rab	15–18	
	Anita	15–18	

Acknowledgments

Grateful acknowledgment is given authors, publishers, and agents for reprinting the following material.

Excerpt from "Winterset" by Maxwell Anderson, copyright 1935 Anderson House and Maxwell Anderson. Published in *Six Modern American Plays,* edited by Allan G. Haline, 1951, Library Edition, Random House, Inc.

Excerpt from "Antigone" by Jean Anouilh, translated by Lewis Galantiere, copyright 1946 by Random House, Inc.

Excerpt from "Campfire" by Marsh Cassady, reprinted by permission of the author. "Campfire" first appeared in *The Theatre and You,* Meriwether Publications, Ltd., Colorado Springs, Colorado. Copyright © 1992 Marsh Cassady.

Excerpt from "The Wrong Man" by Laura Harrington, © 1985 by Laura Harrington. Reprinted by permission of Bret Adams Limited, Artist's Agency, New York City, on behalf of the author. CAUTION: Professionals and amateurs are hereby warned that THE WRONG MAN is subject to a royalty. It is fully protected under the copyright laws of the United States of America, and all countries covered by the International Copyright Union (including the Dominion of Canada and the rest of the British Commonwealth), and of all countries covered by the Pan-American Copyright Convention and the Universal Copyright Convention and of all countries with which the United States has reciprocal copyright relations. All rights, including professional, amateur, motion picture, recitation, lecturing, public reading, radio broadcasting, television, video or sound taping, all other forms of mechanical or electronic reproductions such as information storage and retrieval systems and photocopying, and all rights of translation into foreign languages, are strictly reserved. All inquiries should be addressed to Bret Adams Ltd., 448 West 44th Street, New York, NY 10036, Attention: Mary Harden.

Excerpt from "A Rosen by Any Other Name" by Israel Horovitz, copyright © 1986, and excerpt from "The Chopin Playoffs" by Israel Horovitz, copyright © 1987, reprinted by permission of William Morris Agency, Inc., on behalf of the author. Both plays were originally published in *An Israel Horovitz Trilogy,* 1987, by Nelson Doubleday, Inc.

Excerpt from "Dance and the Railroad" by David Henry Hwang, reprinted by permission of Helen Merrill, Ltd. CAUTION: Professionals and amateurs are hereby warned that DANCE AND THE RAILROAD by David Henry Hwang is fully protected under the Copyright Laws of the United States of America, the British Commonwealth, including the Dominion of Canada, and all other countries of the International Copyright Union and Universal Copyright Convention, and are subject to royalty. All rights, including professional, amateur, motion picture, recitation, lecturing, public reading, radio and television broadcasting and the rights of translation into foreign languages are strictly reserved. Particular emphasis is laid on the question of readings, permission for which must be secured from the author's agent in writing. All inquiries concerning the amateur and professional production rights to DANCE AND THE RAILROAD should be addressed in writing to Helen Merrill, Ltd., 435 West 23rd Street, Suite 1A, New York, NY 10011, USA. No amateur performance or reading of the play may be given without obtaining, in advance, the written permission of Helen Merrill, Ltd. All inquires concerning rights (other than production rights) should also be addressed to Helen Merrill, Ltd.

Excerpt from "FOB," copyright © 1979 by David Henry Hwang, from FOB AND OTHER PLAYS by David Henry Hwang. Used by permission of New American Library, a division of Penguin Books USA Inc.

Excerpt from "My Sister in This House" by Wendy Kesselman. Copyright © 1980 by Wendy Kesselman. Reprinted by permission of the William Morris Agency, Inc., on behalf of the Author. All rights reserved. "My Sister in This House" was first produced by the Actor's Theatre of Louisville, February 1981. CAUTION: Professionals and amateurs are hereby warned that "My Sister in This House" is subject to a royalty. It is fully protected under the copyright laws of the United States of America, and all of the countries covered by the Pan-American Copyright Convention and the Universal Copyright Convention, and of all countries with which the United States has reciprocal copyright relations. All rights, including

Photo credits

NTC SPEECH AND THEATRE BOOKS

Speech Communication
ACTIVITIES FOR EFFECTIVE COMMUNICATION, LiSacchi
THE BASICS OF SPEECH, Galvin, Cooper, & Gordon
CONTEMPORARY SPEECH, HopKins & Whitaker
DYNAMICS OF SPEECH, Myers & Herndon
GETTING STARTED IN PUBLIC SPEAKING, Prentice & Payne
LISTENING BY DOING, Galvin
LITERATURE ALIVE! Gamble & Gamble
MEETINGS: RULES & PROCEDURES, Pohl
PERSON TO PERSON, Galvin & Book
PUBLIC SPEAKING TODAY! Prentice & Payne
SELF-AWARENESS, Ratliffe & Herman
SPEAKING BY DOING, Buys, Sill, & Beck

Theatre
ACTING AND DIRECTING, Grandstaff
THE BOOK OF CUTTINGS FOR ACTING & DIRECTING, Cassady
THE BOOK OF SCENES FOR ACTING PRACTICE, Cassady
THE DYNAMICS OF ACTING, Snyder & Drumsta
AN INTRODUCTION TO MODERN ONE-ACT PLAYS, Cassady
AN INTRODUCTION TO THEATRE AND DRAMA, Cassady & Cassady
NTC's DICTIONARY OF THEATRE AND DRAMA TERMS, Mobley
PLAY PRODUCTION TODAY! Beck et al.
STAGECRAFT, Beck

 For a current catalog and information about our complete line
of language arts books, write:
National Textbook Company,
a division of NTC Publishing Group
4255 West Touhy Avenue
Lincolnwood (Chicago), Illinois 60646-1975 U.S.A.